THE PHANTOM TRAIN
AND OTHER GHOSTLY LEGENDS OF COLORADO

BY

F. DEAN SNEED

ISBN 0-922863-04-0

Designed and published by:
Dream Weavers Publishing Co.
7580 W. 16th St. Suite 325
Lakewood, CO 80215

This book is about the ghosts and haunted houses of early Denver and other towns in Colorado. All the stories, unless otherwise noted, first appeared in the Rocky Mountain News, between the years 1879 and 1894. Most, if not all, haven't seen the light of day in well over one hundred years.

You will find some of the tales to be humorous, some sad and some have a scary moment or two. But, whatever the case, all are entertaining and will help to enrich the already colorful history of this great state.

F. Dean Sneed

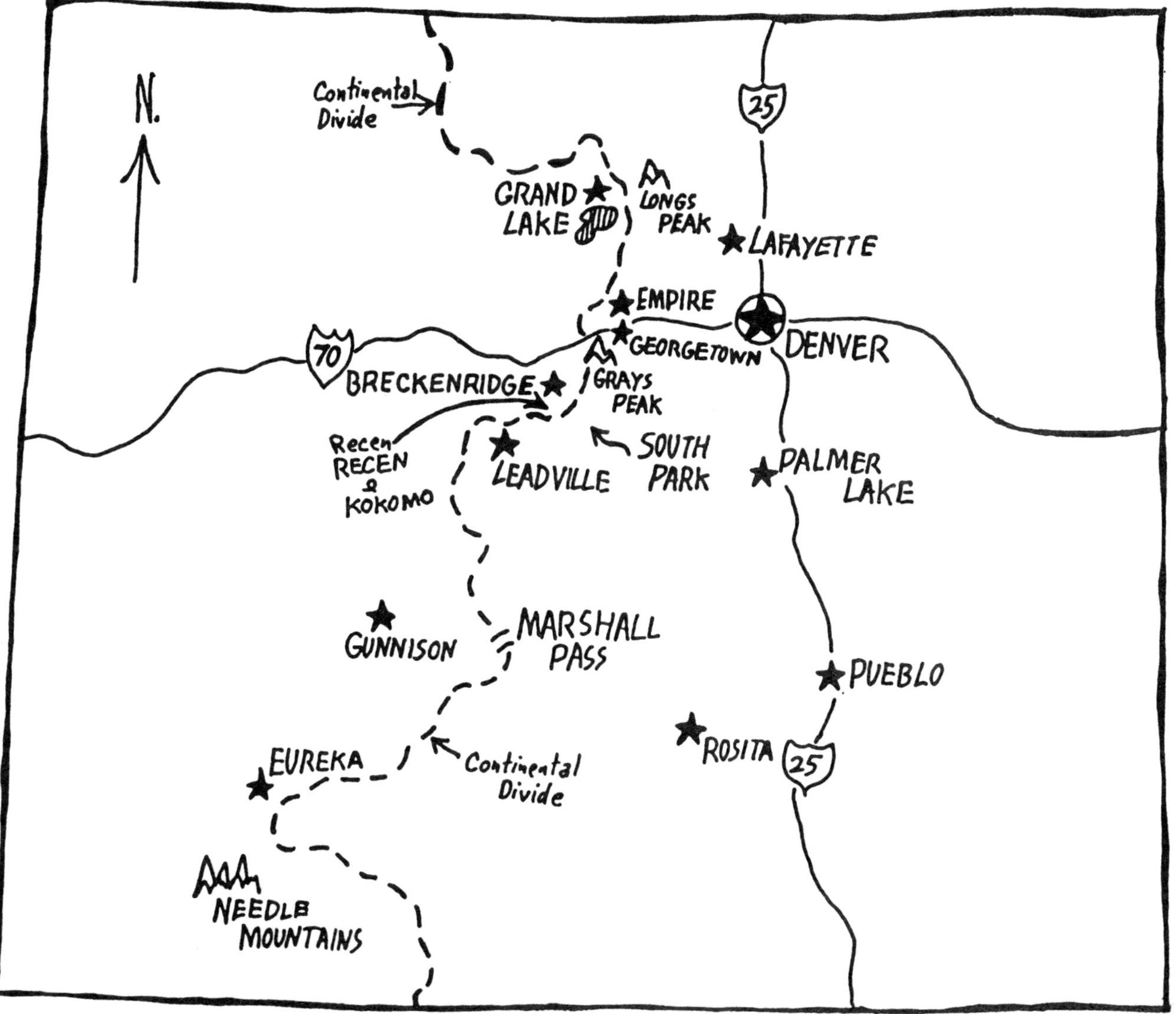

MY THANKS to the Rocky Mountain News, Colorado State Historical Society, the Denver Public Library - Western History Department, and friends and relatives too numerous to mention. This book wouldn't have been possible without their help and patience.

Dean

A HOUSE WHOSE EVERY BRICK IS A TOMB

In one of the pleasantest quarters and loveliest nooks in Denver, there is a house whose quaint beauty and charming surroundings attract more attention and comment than any other place in the city. It has been in existence during a very few years, but has an air of antiquity that makes it seem to have been standing for a century. The herbage and shrubbery has a weird and unnatural appearance that makes the place attractive to the sight, but repels familiarity. This peculiarity is of a character that excites one's curiosity to stroll through the grounds, but while doing so, there is in us a constant feeling of dread and disposition to get away from it, which urges the visitor to move as if some impending danger was following or haunting their steps. The walls of the house are covered in many places completely by trailing vines, whose unnatural green hues startle those who look on the peculiar shades and tone and character of it's color.

Over all these shadowy and strange outlines of vegetation there seems to harbor a lurid and ghostly light, whose rays give to the dullest vision and mind a sense that there is something supernatural harboring about and pervading the mysterious place. The very appearance of old age, which so evidently a new place has taken on, in itself arouses in the beholder a feeling that some spell is on it and its environments, and an involuntary idea possesses us that it is haunted. From this feeling no one escapes. The firmest unbeliever in superstitions, and the dullest and most stupid visitor who lingers thereabouts are alike affected by the weird character of the surroundings, and experience a sense of relief when they get away from the touch and glamour which is entangled in every loop and filament of the vines and branches.

Those who have lived in the house speak with bated breath and hesitation concerning their experiences there. No one has endured a month within it's walls, and the strangest part of the whole story is that none of those who have resided there are able to tell intelligently what caused them to become so uneasy, or why they could not stay. Everyone, however, has a vague idea that it is haunted, and say so in a hesitating sort of way. But they never heard any startling noises, nor have they been disturbed by losses of property, only sleeplessness and faint perceptions of shrouded forms flitting about and around them, and vague feelings that seemed to indicate that something of a supernatural life and character surrounded them. As they found freedom from all this by removing from the place, it is evident that some local cause produces the phenomenon.

These things having been whispered about in an uncertain and indefinite way for some years, at last excited the attention of an investigator, whose courage has always been equal to every emergency to which he has been exposed during many years of his adventurous life. Being determined to investigate the matter on Thursday evening, he went to the place to remain during the night, and as the premises have been abandoned for some months, and no tenant can be induced to endure it's mysteries, he had no difficulty in effecting entrance. The night was peculiarly propitious, as there was lunar light until after midnight, and our readers will remember the moon had a peculiar red and baleful color and singular expression during the entire period of it's presence in the sky. This gave to the house and surroundings a strange and mystical appearance, which would have appalled any other less courageous investigator.

Seating himself in the shadow and angle of the wall, our hero awaited the

sensation of being scared, and he did not have to wait long, for as if aware of his presence, the exhibition of curious scenes soon commenced. At first, it seemed as if the movements that began in a faint way to change the shadows into most grotesque shapes, were caused by the wind toying with tendrils of vines and flowers. But directly they took on apparently tangible form and moved about and around the premises, some with a serpent hissing-like sound, and other with sibilant kisses as if the leaves had lips and were pleasantly using them in a delicious pastime. These fantastic shapes became more numerous and had plainly visible human countenances. Some were stout, athletic-looking creatures, with eyes that shone as of the vaporous forms were living, strong persons, but endowed with ethereal and aerial characteristics that made them intangible. These people flitted to and fro, seeming to be holding a flying convention, yet the only sounds heard were the sighings as of wearied persons, and flutterings as of hovering wings, or light bodies in motion. The forms harbored mostly under the eaves and attached themselves to the bricks of the walls, whence their faces peered like eldritch figures and stared with glowing eyes, that glared as if they looked from stones. Others seemed like petrifications of ghastly wounds.

One form of lovely and ethereal mould seemed the only feminine shade that harbored there, and our gallant hero, true to his instincts and customs, paid attention to her alone. It soon became evident to him that she saw his interest, and began with coyness and hesitation to approach him. Flitting from tree to tree and point to point, he saw her come, now looking dreamily through a framework of leaves, and glance wearily through a loop in the lace-like tracing of vines and lattice-bound flowers that make the place so picturesque.

But now she whispered to him, and in silence he listened to a tale of blood that made him close his eyes with horror. Briefly she told how a jealous lover, who was a workman on that building, had murdered her, and placing her body in the wall had built around her the chimney place in which she was now entombed. But what about these other faces that seem to hover about and harbor on those walls and within the ghostly precincts of the house?

To these questions she answered that the dirt composing the bricks had been taken from an old graveyard, in which hundreds of the victims of greed for gold had been buried since the days of Coronado, who first planted there his dead Spaniards. The spirits of those resent the uses to which the clay of their bodies have been applied, and thus harbor on the walls and about the house, and will always make it untenable while that condition of sacrilege exists. Looking up and around the place, her auditor saw many faces turned toward him, sad eyes longingly and wistfully expressing the hope that was in their thus fettered souls. Wondering and doubting, he looked his inquiry again, and;

She, divining his questioning heart, said:

"There are ghosts that walk the earth and are never laid.

Attendant through your mundane strife, the dear immortal spirits tread,

The boundless universe is life, In earth or sky there are no dead."

On Friday an investigation was made, and in the recess of the wall, as described, the skeleton of the murdered girl was found. After a careful investigation of the matter, it has been considered prudent to give no further publicity until the assassin is secured, which event may be hoped for ere long, as he still lives, and strange to tell, often visits here and lingers in the vicinity of his fearful crime.

June 29, 1879

Reprinted with the permission of the Rocky Mountain News

Since a follow-up story was not recorded, the fate of both the house and the murderer is unknown and will probably remain so.

It is hoped, however that the sad spirits of the bricks and vines have finally found the peace they so deserve. It is also hoped that the "assassin" was eventully brought to justice; if not in this world, then in the next.

A TRAGIC TALE

A Bloody Reminiscence of Early Denver
The Killing of Fitzgibbons by Tenney in '66.
A House Which Acquired a Spirit as the Result.

Old timers recollect many events about Denver localities that are as wild and at the same time as true as any to be found in the history of any part of the world. There are some sections of the city where it is said the houses are built over secret graveyards. Strange and horrible crimes were perpetrated in the early days of the Queen City. Men disappeared from the community and no record of their whereabouts has ever come to light, while deeds of violence were committed which were not discovered till months, and in some cases, years afterward. There were probably fewer of these wild deeds in 1858 and 1859 than at a period five or ten years afterward. The old timers always claim that there were few criminals in very early days, that the tenderfeet *furnished most of the early criminals.*

It was in the year 1866 that an event occurred that has probably faded out of many men's minds. A man named Gerald Fitzgibbons came here the year before from Texas. He was no longer a young man, but was still a vigorous and fiery individual. He did not settle on the then flourishing West Side of the town, but built a pretty good frame house for that day on a portion of Arapahoe street, which was then but sparsely populated.

Fitzgibbons had evidently led a pretty wild life, and his having been a sort of a guerilla in the confederate service rather worked against him in those days, when the old spirit ran high and sectional feeling had by no means passed away. Fitzgibbons, who was a man with a fierce black moustache and whose remaining hair, which clung to either side of his other-wise bald crown, made no secret of his political principles and did not attempt to disguise the fact that he had been guilty of acts outside of his war records which would have been equally condemned both at North and South. He was fond of being considered a bad man and told many wild and blood curdling stories of the incidents in his career. He started a saloon on the other side of the creek which was fairly well patronized.

About this time, a young, light complexioned, smooth faced man came into Denver. He carried on his left side an empty sleeve and had served in the Northern army. Rather delicate in his features and fragile in his general appearance, it was a wonder to the early Denverites that he could drink so much whiskey and not act in all respects like a "thoroughbred". His name was Walter H. Tenney and he was as fierce a unionist as the Texan was a confederate. As soon as the two became acquainted it was easy to see that the Denver of that day was not large enough to long hold both of them.

Tenney was better read in history than Fitzgibbons was and was able, in the opinion of the citizens at least, to get the better of the Texan in argument. The latter had more than once *threatened his life* ....and one night had grossly insulted him. Tenney replied, but not with a pistol shot. He leveled his remaining right arm at Fitzgibbons' stomach and knocked him down. Fitzgibbons rose thoroughly mad, but before he could get at his hip pocket, Tenney gave him a hard blow in the face which knocked him senseless. By the advice of his friends, Tenney, who was tolerably sober, left the saloon. When Fitzgibbons came to his senses he swore that he would have the young man's life, but the latter, whether from prudence or cowardice, avoided his place. Recollection of the assault and of Fitzgibbons' threats had faded out in the public mind, as there was *a new mining excitement* springing up, and men were leaving for the new camp. It was about ten days after the events in the saloon that a Denver man, who was passing Fitzgibbons' place at an early hour in the morning, was attracted by a low moan that sounded strangely human in its cadence.

The citizen found the door of the saloon unlocked and went in. Fitzgibbons was found just inside the bar, lying on his face and bleeding from a wound in the side. A physician was called in and with some assistance the man was restored to partial consciousness, and the wound dressed and examined. Fitzgibbons gave the name of Tenney as his assailant. He said the latter had induced him to open the saloon and give him a drink. Tenney appeared pretty drunk. Fitzgibbons' sense of honor would not permit him to take advantage of a man in Tenney's condition, and though he used some pretty strong language toward his late enemy, he attempted no violence. While he was mixing a cocktail, however, Tenney, quick as lightning, presented a pistol and fired. Some of the glassware at the back of the bar was shattered, but no one was harmed.

Fitzgibbons being thoroughly aroused, jumped over the bar and exclaimed, "You cowardly son of a ________, I'll kill you for this". The two grappled in a hand to hand conflict and Fitzgibbons tried to knock Tenney in the head with the butt of a revolver. He suddenly felt that in the scuffle he had been

stabbed and dropped to the floor unconscious. Tenney had apparently fled after committing the deed, and he was never again heard of in Denver. Fitzgibbons lingered along a few days and died.

The house where he breathed his last was vacant for several years, but was finally taken up by a newly arrived tenderfoot and his family. They occupied it only about two months and left it under the impression *that it was haunted.*

The occupant, whose name was Peter Smith, declared that he had heard noises as of men scuffling and that they were followed by low moans as of a wounded man. His family confirmed these stories. The real estate man who took the house abused Smith roundly for injuring the value of the property. It was several years before it was sold again, and the family who came to occupy it left in a hurry, believing that they had, several times, seen a tall Texan moving about in the night. The apparition always appeared *with a wound in its side* .

Some years ago the house took fire and was burned, and, strange to say, the lot where it stood still remains vacant. As for the saloon property, it was owned at different times by several parties, and the owners and lessees always found it a profitless task to attempt to carry it on. Burglars robbed it several times, and like the haunted house it was at length destroyed, being swept away by a Cherry Creek flood.

These incidents gain a new interest from the fact that a prominent Denver physician, who wishes his name withheld, has lately found an old manuscript among a deceased physician's effects which appears to be a confession by one Dr. Alf Smith, who says he was the one who attended Fitzgibbons in his last moments. The latter confessed that he had a scuffle with Tenney in his (Fitzgibbons') own house a few nights preceding the stabbing in the saloon. Tenney had come to him boldly and asked for a compromise on the ground that he knew some doings of Fitzgibbons' in Texas that would have, even at that late day, sent him to the penitentiary. He shot at Tenney, but the latter had escaped. Fitzgibbons made the doctor promise to keep the secret through life, but had confessed on his death bed.   He also told a rather wild story of a man whom he always believed to be Tenney called at his house one night seeking professional services. The man, however, denied being Tenney and and said that he had only just come to Denver.

The above circumstances are vouched for by old timers and forms one of the many interesting episodes that marked the earlier history of the city.

December 25, 1883

Reprinted with the permission of the Rocky Mountain News

SPIRIT SHOES

Spirit Shoes
How They Glide About a Skating Rink at Night
Something For the Materialists to Explain if They Can

The bright rays of the gentle moon were bathing, in their soft effulgence, the roofs and towers of the sleeping town. The only persons abroad at the unseemly hour were policeman, reporters and other questionable characters.

The day had been an eventful one, marking as it did the opening of the new skating rink.[1] Manager Bush had retired to his couch in an excited state that precluded all attempts at slumber. His restlessness increased so that after many ineffectual attempts to woo the drowsy god he arose, dressed himself and, moved by an impulse that he could not resist, he strolled around the vicinity of the rink. As he slowly sauntered past the door a sound greeted his ears that made him stop, *almost rooted to the earth.* He listened again and heard distinctly the sound of roller skates making the round of the large pavilion. Yet the skaters had gone hours ago. With a curiosity not unmixed with fear he struck a match, and applying his key to the lock of the door, he slowly opened it and to his amazement discovered the place illuminated by a lurid light that seemed to penetrate the remotest portion of the interior with its ghastly effulgence.

A sight still more strange than this greeted his astonished vision. There, gliding along with a swiftness incredible and a skill seemingly unattainable were two pairs of human feet encased in an equal number of Pumpton rollers, and both keeping time to the strains of ghostly music. With a terror-stricken glance the dazed manager sought in vain to discover the bodies of *these apparition feet.*

After a time, his fear subsided somewhat, he made a closer examination of the pedals, and to his great astonishment recognized in one pair those of the great treasurer, J. Cook, Jr.[2] This he did partially by their great size and partially by the impress of a particular favorite corn in the number ten boot. The other pair, however, were much smaller and were of dainty kid, undoubtedly those of a lady. After gazing in a sort of horrified trance for some time, the unearthly music ceased, the light disappeared and all was silent.

Filled with wonder and amazement at the sight he had witnessed he at once proceeded to the residence of the Napoleonic treasurer on Broadway, and after, with

16

with considerable difficulty awakening him, told him the strange story. As soon as Cook fully comprehended the purport, he said, "I have been quite restless ever since retiring and have had strange dreams and when you awoke me, I discovered that my feet, which I always have great difficulty in keeping covered, were outside the bed and as cold as ice." Both the manager and the treasurer will consult eminent spiritual and clairvoyant authority at the first opportunity in an endeavor to obtain a solution of the strange phenomenon.

FORMER LOCATION OF THE DENVER SKATING RINK

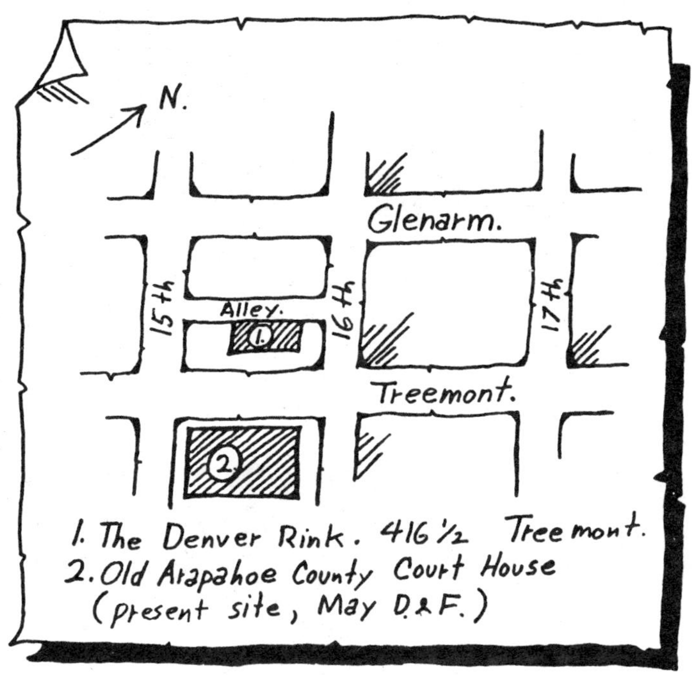

February 10, 1884

Reprinted with the permission of the Rocky Mountain News.

1. Refers to the "Denver Rink", 391 (416 1/2) Tremont Street. Opened in 1884, the rink apparently didn't do very well, for within three years it was already abandoned. The building was to remain empty until 1901, when W.B. Felker purchased the property with the intention of constructing a "general automobile business" on the site. Today all trace of the rink is gone and the land is now being used as a parking lot.
2. J. Cook Jr.; Noted Denver real-estate man and treasurer for "The Organization of the Colorado game and Fish Protective Asso." (1882)

GHOST OR GOBLIN

A Woman in White
Seen in the Alley Near the Dissecting Room. [1]
Adventure of a Man
Who Tried to Capture the Midnight Prowler.
The Ghost
Recognized as an Old- Time Denver Vagrant.

A man giving his name as Jake Dellman, a blacksmith by trade, met a NEWS reporter yesterday and asked him if he believed in ghosts.

"No, I do not. Why do you ask?" was the response to the interrogatory.

"Well, I do. I didn't until last night, but I am satisfied now that they exist."

"What proved it to you?"

"My own eyes. I have seen one for the past three nights. I'll tell you how it was. Tuesday night I had been uptown until late and stopped at the post-office[2] to mail some letters. I lived on the West Side and thought I would take a shortcut through the alley when something white flitted past me and crouched close beside a brick wall on the right side of the alley. I wasn't frightened at all but marched up to the figure, which ran away from me and disappeared suddenly on Fourteenth Street.

I went on home thinking about the occurrence and the next night I determined to go through the alley again. I passed through it several times and seeing nothing, concluded it was too early, and went uptown to wait until it was later. About midnight I went down Larimer Street, intending to go up Fourteenth Street. When opposite Mr. Walley's undertaking establishment[3] I saw the same white figure I had seen the night before standing ***near the vacant building*** on the corner of Fourteenth.

The figure was standing perfectly quiet and was plainly visible by the rays of the electric light. I stepped into the doorway of the building formerly occupied by Mitchell & Bros.[4] as a cigar store, which is now vacant, as is the store room adjoining, and watched the woman in white. I saw her, very plainly, glide along Fourteenth, walk as far as the alley and disappear. I ran after her and went through the alley to Fifteenth Street but could see no sign of the spook. I turned around and walked through the alley again, and when near the same place I saw the

same figure again, which disappeared in the same manner. I waited around for half an hour or so trying to catch another glimpse of my ghost but left, thinking the police might spot me as a suspicious character."

"What was it you saw?"

"A woman, bare-footed and bare-headed, with a sheet wrapped around her."

"Are you sure of it?"

"Certainly I am. I was in ten feet of her once, and could see everything but her face. I wasn't satisfied, however, and went back the next night."

"Did you see her?"

"Hold on until I tell the whole thing. I stayed over home until 11:30 o'clock, and started downtown expecting to reach the trysting place of the woman. I wasn't satisfied that it was a spirit ... at exactly midnight, the time good ghosts are expected to walk. I stopped in the shadow of the Chamber of Commerce[5.] and waited for ten minutes longer, but didn't see anything. I walked up and down across the alley entrance for ten minutes longer, but saw nothing. I went through the alley *but saw nothing.*"

"I loitered for perhaps a quarter of an hour on Fifteenth Street and went through the alley again. When about half way through, I saw the same white figure. It had its back to me and seemed to be crouched close against the wall. I went forward noiselessly, determined to spring on and capture it if I got close enough to jump."

"Did you?"

"Don't get excited. I got within six feet of the object and jumped. I caught something in my arms. I don't know what it was for it vanished the moment I saw it, but as suddenly reappeared ten feet away. I got a good look at the face, however, and recognized it."

"Who was it?"

"Lizzie Greer."[6.]

"Are you sure?"

"Of course I am. I knew her well when she was alive and saw her at the coroner's after she died. She didn't look any different, except that she was somewhat cleaner than she was in the flesh."

"Did you see her anymore that night?"

"As I said, when she evaporated out of my arms she reappeared ten feet distant. I went toward her, but she again disappeared. I would go and look for her tonight, but it is a little too cold. I don't see how Liz stands it with nothing on but a sheet."**

** THE FOLLOWING DAY, DECEMBER 13, 1885, THIS BIZARRE
FOLLOW-UP STORY APPEARED.

**An Undertaker's Assistant Anxious to Catch Lizzie Greer.
He Thinks She Has No Business Wandering Around of Nights.
He is Determined to Catch Her and Plant Her Again.**

"I had a queer experience a little while ago," said Mr. Dellman to a NEWS reporter about 2 o'clock this morning.

"Did you see Liz Greer again?"

"No, but I was looking for her and ran into another man who was doing the same thing."

"He must have read your experience in this morning's paper."

"That is just exactly what he did, or at least, his boss did and sent him out to investigate. The fellow was an undertaker's assistant and had horse and wagon standing nearby, and was prowling up and down the alley courageously, in hopes of coming across poor Lizzie's ghost, which he would attempt to lay out, and if he succeeded, would plank her in the wagon, haul her to the undertaking establishment, give it out that another pauper had died and charge the county for burying her."

"I don't understand you exactly."

"When a pauper dies, the undertaker who buries her gets so much from the county; $2.50 I believe it is. Of course that wouldn't pay him, but if he can sell the subject to a dissecting room for $30, he will come out alright and get his coffin back. The same coffin can be used for innumerable subjects that way, and the undertaker instead of losing money by burying a pauper actually makes money."

"But are pauper subjects sold to the medical fraternity?"

"Those that are not sold are resurrected and used in the dissecting room. But that isn't what I started to tell. I hovered around the alley about midnight , expecting to meet my old friend Liz, but instead of meeting her, I met this fellow every time, and finally asked him his business. Of course, he asked mine, but by dint of perseverance and tact I got him to tell his story.

He said his boss had told him that it was reported that Liz Greer was still alive and was in the habit of haunting that alley, and his orders were to capture her if he had to knock her in the head and put her in the coffin.

I asked him if he wasn't afraid and he said that he didn't know whether he was or not, but he was satisfied of one thing; if she went traipsing through that alley while he was around he was going to capture and make her stay dead. He said he knew she was dead, for he had seen her laid out, but there was so many people come to life after dying that she might be one of them. Finally a bright idea seemed to strike him. He said he would know her anyhow, for she didn't have but one leg. When I inquired what he meant by that he said he saw one of her legs cut off, and if she went running through that alley with more than one leg he would shoot her, for he'd know **she was a ghost, then**. "

"Did he see her?"

"I don't think he did. I left him just a few minutes ago. He hadn't then, and as I heard a wagon drive off shortly after, I suppose he didn't. The fool was armed with a big revolver and a policeman's club and he was determined, if the ghost walked, to give it a chase. He was sent out to get a stiff and he was going to have one, if it could be found."

"Liz didn't walk tonight, then?"

"No, she didn't, and I am afraid that fool has spoiled my chances for an investigation. She evidently knows him and has no desire to be planted again, which is the reason she kept out of his way. I am pursuing my researches merely to satisfy my curiosity. That fellow thinks if he can capture her, he will make a dollar or two for his boss. Well, he shan't have her as long as I am around. I'll tell you what I'll do. Tomorrow night we will both get an interview out of her about the dissecting room. I am inclined to think she knows all about it. You can get her to tell you everything that has occurred after she died. It will be interesting."

December 13, 1885

Reprinted with the permission of the Rocky Mountain News.

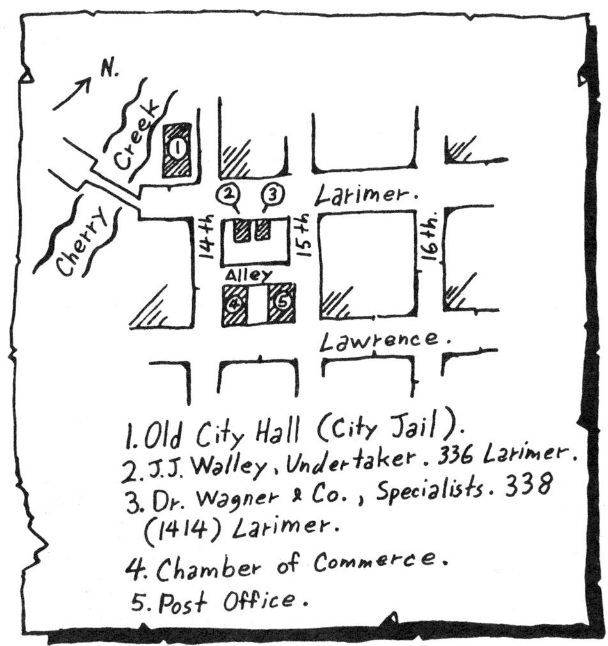

1. Probably refers to "Dr. Wagner & Co., Specialists" 338 (1414) Larimer Street. A favorite hangout of medical students. The establishment was also known as "The Corpse Corral."

2. Post Office, 15th and Lawrence St. Present site of "Lawrence Court".

3. J. J. Walley, Undertaker, 336 Larimer St. Conveniently located next to "Dr. Wagner & Co."

4. Listed only as "Mitchell & Bros., Larimer" (Denver City Directory, 1885).

5. Chamber of Commerce, Northeast corner of 14th and Lawrence St.

6. An obituary, of sorts, ran in the Denver Republican on January 6, 1881. It pretty much tells it all:

An Unfortunate Fallen

Lizzie Greer Follows Jeanie Murruy (?) to the Hospital.

The old time Denverites well remember Lizzie Greer, at one time the leader of the Demi-Monde. She came to Denver from Louisville, where she had been a great favorite and made much money. Her diamonds were the marvel of the city and her wardrobe was the most extensive and costly in the city. Her note was as readily done at the banks as that of the most successful business man. Her career, though wicked, was brilliant. She reached the zenith of her fame in 1861 and 1862. From that time on her decline had been gradual but sure. Her beauty, which was unadorned and notorious, faded; her money disappeared; her admirers deserted her. To drown her sorrows she resorted to drink. Her fall was complete. For several years she has lived a wretched sort of life in the byways and alleys of the city, purchasing liquor by the tin-pail full at low groggeries and subsisting on the offals found in rear of hotels and restaurants. Lately, she has lived in a hovel in the sand on the platte bottoms, occasionally receiving aid from old friends and admirers who chanced to meet her. On Tuesday night she slept in Lewis and Wheelers lumber yard, Ninteenth and Blake Sts. Yesterday she was removed from the vicinity of the lumber yard by officer Minehart and taken to the County Hospital. The end is not far distant.

THE DEATH OF "DUTCH ANNIE"

Annie Busch, an Insane Woman, Hangs Herself In Her Cell.
The City Jail the Scene of a Desperate Woman's Fatal Drop.
The Coroner Take Charge of the Body and Decides to Hold No Inquest.

Annie Busch known as "Dutch Annie" was found hanging, dead, in cell no.1, city jail,[1] yesterday morning about 7 o'clock. Annie had been in several days and was locked up for safe-keeping; she had been considered insane.

Night jailer Murray was absent Wednesday night on account of sickness in his family and Officer John Connors was detained in his place. About 4 o'clock Mr. Connors passed her cell and she made some request of him, but in such a manner that he could not understand her. At 7:15 Officer Connors, assisted by a trustee, a big colored man, named Bill Black, started on his rounds to give the prisoners their breakfast. He noticed when they reached Annie's door that she seemed to be standing up against it, and when he opened it she lurched forward, without falling, however, and he did not know that she had hanged herself until the door was swung clear open. He saw that **she was suspended from** the top grating by a towel. He immediately ordered the trustee, Bill Black, to bring him  a knife. The fellow was scared so badly that he let fall all the dishes he had in his hands and ran away. The officer procured a knife himself and cut the body down, endeavoring to find signs of life, but failed.

The coroner was summoned and removed the remains to his undertaking rooms, from where she will be buried. No inquest will be held.

When placed in jail, Annie had four new towels, and two of these were used in her self-destruction. She removed the strings from her corset and laid them lengthwise in two towels which she had tied together. The whole was then twisted into a rope, one end of which she tied around her neck and the other around a bar in the upper part of the door, having to stand upon the iron cot in the cell to reach it. When everything was adjusted she either jumped from the bed or pushed it from her. The rope stretched so that she could have touched the floor with the tips of her toes and sustained life, but she had **deliberately bent her knees** drawing her feet up several inches from the floor, and in that position she was found.

December 30, Annie was taken to jail on the complaint of the people with whom she lived, on the corner of Nineteenth and Larimer Street. They claimed that she was crazy and that they feared she would set the house afire. She was flighty and seemed to be under the impression that someone was going to harm her. Dr. McLauthlin was called and administered a sedative to the woman.

The next day she was so much better that she was released. The night of January 4, as assistant jailer McLean was going home, he met Annie on the corner of Fourteenth and Larimer streets. She was very much excited and begged McLean not to let anyone hurt her, as several threatened to kill her. She said she had no place to go and unless protected she would certainly be killed. McLean sent her to police headquarters and she was sent to jail as a sleeper. Dr. McLauthlin was summoned. He gave her a hypodermic injection of morphine and she fell asleep.

The next day she was violent whenever the jailer approached her, exclaiming that she was **guilty of violating the law** and said it was the fault of the fortune teller, alluding to an old woman on Nineteenth Street, who makes a practice of predicting the future for women who are silly enough to visit her. During her stay in jail until she ended her life the woman ate nothing of any consequence, did not sleep, and was really sick. Jailers Brady and McLean say that she should have been sent to the county hospital, and would have been taken there had she not been refused admittance.

Though the woman was called "Dutch Annie", it is claimed she was French and did not even know the German language. She had been in Denver for several years plying her vocation and was not considered a bad woman of her class. She was about 25 years old and not ill-looking in face or figure. From all account had she been placed in a hospital, where she rightly belonged, she could have been cured of her malady. There is another woman in jail, who in slang parlance, is off her nut, and if she is not looked after is liable to go the same way as Annie.

IN A FOLLOW-UP STORY, ANNE APPARENTLY REAPPEARS AS A GHOST AND HAUNTS THE CITY JAIL ------------------>

A Ghost in the Jail.
Annie Busch, the Woman Who Hanged Herself,
Re-visits Her Old Quarters.

"There are queer goings on here of night", said Mr. Sam Murray, the night jailer at the city jail to NEWS reporter last night, as he stood warming at the heater.

"What is it now, tramps bother you?"

"No. I've got a ghost now. A regular spook. I haven't said anything about it before for fear of being laughed at."

"I suppose Annie Busch[2] has come back and haunts the building."

"That's just what it is. She is here or was here tonight. I haven't seen her myself but several of the prisoners have, and I have had a curious feeling come over several times which made me believe something unearthly was about. Last night one of the trustees went to the cell where she hung herself to give a woman who was in there a drink of water. When he reached the cell he dropped the cup and ran away yelling. I asked him the cause and he told me there were two women in that cell, and one of them was Annie Busch. I couldn't induce him to go back to the cell."

"He had the jim-jams."

"No, he didn't. I believe he saw her. I asked the girl if she saw anybody in the cell. She said she hadn't, but that she felt someone near all the night, and that it had really made her sick. I placed her in another cell."

"When did Annie start making her visits?"

"The night after she hung herself some of the prisoners asked me why I didn't lock up that woman and stop her running round through the corridors. I didn't know what to say. I supposed they were guying me until Henry Miller, one of the prisoners told me he had seen Annie Busch. The next night it was the same way, and her visits have been kept up since."

"What does she do in her nocturnal rambles?"

"Flits around the jail from one place to another, always disappearing in cell no.1, where she killed herself. A funny thing about this whole thing is that she has never paid me a personal visit."

The reporter spoke to a number of the prisoners and all claimed that there was a woman who flitted around the jail at night, but they didn't know whether she was a ghost or not. They were inclined to think she wasn't. Annie Busch, the woman whose ghost is said to visit the jail, hanged herself to a cell door about two weeks ago. She had been demented for some time previous. Whether her ghost visits the jail or not, something supernatural in the shape of a woman does, and nothing but a complete investigation by the police will satisfy the jailer and his pets.

January 20, 1886

Reprinted with the permission of the Rocky Mountain News.

1. City Jail, 14th and Larimer St. - All that remains of the jail (part of the old City Hall), is a small park and a large bell. On its base is a plaque which reads:

This bell

is the only existing relic

of Denver old city hall.

Built on this site in 1883

and razed in 1936.

2. It should be noted that Annie busch not only haunted the jail, but was also seen near the infamous "Corpse Corral". Her body had been taken there after her death. Whether she and Liz Greer went out haunting together is not known.

A NIGHT OF HORROR

The Terrible Story
Told by a Denver Man of One Night's Experience in a Haunted House.
The Undefinable Feeling
Which Took Possession of Him While Quietly Sitting Reading at a Table.
After Retiring to Sleep
He is Awakened By a Sensation of Horror Which Paralyzes Every Faculty.
He Witnesses a Ghastly Tragedy
Which Was Enacted in the Room Before His Very Eyes.

"I had always disbelieved in ghosts", said Mr. Charles Wharton, an old timer and a gentleman of intelligence and good judgement, to a NEWS reporter yesterday, "until a terrible experience which I had several years ago, rather destroyed my skepticism and made me an unwilling believer in the supernatural, that the spirits, particularly of those who met violent deaths and might be supposed from any cause to rest uneasy in their graves would re-visit the earth, and especially haunt the scenes of their last residence on earth in the flesh. The one event to which I allude with all of its horrible details, has been burned into my memory as with a hot iron in such startling characters as to ever present with me, sleeping or waking, in all it's hideousness".

Thinking the ***usually well-balanced mind*** of Mr. Wharton was wandering, his listener gazed on him with a surprised, questioning look. Seeing which, the gentleman said, "I see you think I am insane upon a subject which has turned the brain of many a strongminded man, but if you will listen to my story, you will at least give me credit for my present sanity after what I've witnessed and experienced.

It was in the spring of 1881, just after the adjournment of the legislature of that year, with which I was connected, that I concluded to permanently reside in Denver, and sought for comfortable rooms within easy distance of the business portion. It was after several days search during which I examined pretty nearly every furnished apartment that was to let within the bounds that I had set and I had about made up

my hand to look further toward the suburbs when a friend informed me that he knew of a pleasant suite of rooms on Champa Street that would probably suit me. I thanked him and at once proceeded to the place indicated.

I found a neat ***modest looking, two-storied cottage***, standing some distance back from the street and almost hidden by trees and foliage. An air of quiet and contentment and almost rural beauty surrounded the place, and at a glance I was convinced even from the exterior that the quarters would suit me. Opening the gate I walked up the long and well kept path and knocked at the door. The summons was answered by an old lady, with a look that was at once kindly and hospitable, but upon whose face there were lines seemingly produced more by some great sorrow than by the simple ravages of time. Ascertaining that my information was correct as to the rooms being vacant, I was conducted by the old lady to the second floor, where I was shown two comfortable, pleasant front rooms, facing the street, with a small shaded veranda in front, to which access was had from one of the long windows which extended to the floor.

The rooms were pleasant and cheerful, with ***nothing peculiar about them***, and were neatly furnished. They communicated with each other by a door on the center of the partition wall. The terms, which were very moderate, were readily acceded to by me, and after designating the larger of the two as the one I wished for my bed chamber, meaning to use the other as a dressing room and study, I departed to the hotel and had my luggage removed to my new quarters at once, congratulating myself on my good luck in securing such comfortable quarters.

I returned to my new home about 9 o'clock in the evening, arranged the fire in the little grate in the smaller room and sat down quietly to read. I had become greatly interested in Bulwer and his weird stories of mesmerism and the will force, but only in a curious way, and not that they had any effect in influencing my mind or imagination. I had read for perhaps two hours, when I felt rather than saw that ***I was not alone***.

Something was in the room with me, but what it was I could not imagine. I looked up, but could see nothing save the old-fashioned pictures on the wall and the few articles of furniture in the room. The lamp had burned somewhat low, and the blaze of the soft coal in the grate flickered in a fitful sort of a way, casting peculiar shadows on the wall. Taking the lamp and turning up the wick somewhat, I proceeded to examine the fastenings of the doors and windows in both rooms, and found them all secure. Then every nook and corner of the apartments were searched, but nothing reward the effort. Thinking the sensation for it was neither sight nor sound that had disturbed me, but a vagary of the brain superinduced perhaps by the book I was reading, I again sat down, resolved not to be again the victim of my imagination.

I hadn't been seated very long before I again experienced the same sensation accompanied by the soft rustle of a dress. Looking up instantly I imagined I saw the outlines of a form ***disappearing in the wall*** opposite. After a time recovering somewhat from the excitement, although my pulse still beat faster than usual. I tried to persuade myself that I was the victim of a delusion and settled myself again to my book, but I could not concentrate my faculties on the page before me and resolved to go to bed. I will confess that upon reaching the bedroom I was impelled to lock the door between the apartments, there being both a lock and bolt on the door. I had soon ensconced myself in the comfortable bed, leaving the light burning on a table near by, but turned down pretty low. After some little while I fell into a troubled sort of slumber. I had slept for perhaps an hour when I awakened with the sensation of a cold, clammy hand being passed over my face. The very blood congealed in my veins as I looked up and saw between the light and the bed the **dim**

outline of a human form , although I could see the light through it. Presently while I looked it gradually receded, passing through the door between the rooms. As soon as I could muster sufficient courage I arose, turned up the lamp and examined the door, but found it fastened as I had left it.

After this experience it was perhaps an hour before I again fell off into a sleep which at the best was a restless, uneasy dream. Suddenly I became thrilled with a feeling of horror too intense for description; every faculty seemed paralyzed with fear. Looking into the center of the room which was illuminated by a pale ghastly light, the oil in the lamp having burned out, I saw a fearful scene enacted. There were the figures of a man and woman, the latter dressed in a white robe, seemingly a night dress, evidently young and, but for the steely, glassy eyes, pretty. The man, who was in full dress, was **dragging her by the hair** through the door from the other room, which stood wide open. With a quick movement he thrust the woman to the floor, and with a glittering knife cut her throat, almost severing the head from the body. Then ensued a series of the most unearthly shrieks and groans, followed by a crash as if the house had fallen in a mass. At this my over strained nerves gave way, and I lay in a deathly swoon, lasting perhaps, for hours. When I finally opened my eyes, the blessed sunlight was shining in the room, and with difficulty I mastered my trembling limbs sufficiently to dress myself. Although it was with a shudder, I managed to summon up courage enough to open the communicating door. Everything in the little room was as I had left it, but on the open page of the book I had been reading **was a drop of blood!**

It is needless to say I sought other quarters that same day, and afterward ascertained that the rooms had never had another occupant, or at least one who stayed more than one night.

Soon the tenant of the other portion of the house moved away and it remained idle for nearly a year when it was torn down to make room for a handsome block. Feeling a curiosity about the old house, I went to look at it on the day it was demolished. Upon tearing down the outer wall the workmen found what appeared to have once been a closet, but which appeared to have been closed up. In the bottom of this receptacle was found the ***skeleton of a woman.***

A slight investigation was made and it was learned that some years before a somewhat notorious character had lived in the house with a young and beautiful wife, of whom he was inordinately jealous. That one day they both disappeared and were not seen or heard of afterward. Since that time the house had changed tenants frequently, until it was torn down. Is it any wonder that after this experience, which made my hair as white as you now see it, and which was the result of that night of terror, that I am a believer in ghosts?"

February 8, 1886

Reprinted with the permission of the Rocky Mountain News.

TWO DENVER SPOOKS

**The Blood-Curdling Experience
of Two Gentlemen Who Would Go Chasing Ghosts.
A Whole House Full
of Restless Wraiths Rehearsing a Famous Tragedy.
The Beetle-Browed Villain
Slays a Lady of Beauteous Mien and Scares Two Observing Mortals.**

A gentleman at present stopping at the Albany[1.] lately told a NEWS represent-
ative a strange and weird story, which is as exciting as it is mysterious. A few years
ago he was in the city, and not desirous of stopping at a hotel, sought a room in a
then quiet neighborhood on Seventeenth Street. The house was spacious, as well as
luxuriously furnished. A massive oak door formed the entrance from the wide
hallway to the parlor, in the rear of which there was a sitting room and library
combined, and directly behind that a dining room, which was connected with a
pantry and kitchen by a narrow passageway, in which a trap-door led to a dark and
poorly ventilated cellar. In the front hall there was a wide, easy staircase, with a
landing halfway, which ascended to the second floor, composed of five rooms, a hall
bedroom, a front sitting room, two side bedrooms and a bathroom. A narrow, steep
pair of stairs led from this latter room to a roughly finished attic.

The landlady, a modest, quiet-appearing woman of middle age, informed the
gentleman that he could occupy the front room upstairs and the hall bedroom, which
were connected by an alcove hung with heavy, spotless white lace. The furniture in
the two rooms was costly and dark, which made the contrast with the pure white
more marked. She informed him in a modest way that if he so desired he could use
the parlor in the evening when he wished to enjoy a smoke.
The privilege of the library was also granted. This latter was
appreciated owing to the choice collection of books and
magazines.

He went down town that evening, a bright summer
night, the moon shining in space and throwing a cold, silvery
light over nature. That night he played several games of
billiards, and at 11 o'clock reached his new home. As he
opened the hall door he noticed that the parlor door was ajar,
and a light burning low in the sitting room. He stepped on the
soft carpets of the parlor, crossed the floor, and pushing aside
the portieres between the two rooms, saw the landlady seated in an easy chair, her
head resting in her hand, her elbow on the chair arm. She glanced up quietly. They
conversed for about a quarter of an hour in low tones, when she arose, and bidding

35

him goodnight, passed upstairs. He lit his cigar and was smoking placidly in that frame of mind so peculiar to the confirmed bachelor, when a strange silence settled over the room, and in the dim gaslight a feeling of awe gradually overcame him. He felt that he was not alone. He shook himself, and throwing his half burned cigar in a china cuspidor, turned out the light. The moonbeams broke softly in through the half-parted lace curtains and danced on the rich carpets in apparent ecstacy of delight. The night was cool, the air sweet and delicious, and with a feeling of satisfaction he closed the parlor door and sank resignedly in a comfortable settee. How long he sat buried in contemplation he did not know.

A cloud passed under the moon and the room was left in total darkness. The wind arose and sighed. He heard the floor in the hallway creak. Paralyzed, he sat upright, his hands clenched to resist unwarranted intrusion. A moment and a light step. The night grew darker, the wind sounded more distant to the nervous watcher. He got up cautiously and stepped forward. At the same instant he heard a dress rustle behind him. His fear left him, and with an evil thought in his mind and blood coursing swiftly through his veins, he turned and was about to speak, when the parlor door noiselessly opened and struck him in the back. With blood congealed and cold chills permeating his back, he reached out his hand. In the darkness his finger-tips came in contact with a velvety something--what? Strange, fantastic forms

flitted hither and thither in darkness. Speechless, he tried to cry out. Riveted to the floor, he could not move. He tried to gaze through the room ....a step on the stairs of the cellar way, the floor creaked significantly and a hoarse whisper, "Wait", startled him. Through the darkness came a faint blue light. How quiet the room! Death-like silence prevailed, and an instant later there burst into full view a woman of dazzling beauty, young, a picture of health, her face dimpled in a sweet, childish smile. "Good evening stranger." her voice was soft and low and with a winning smile, the vision stepped forward and motioned the startled smoker to a seat on a soft chair. Surprised beyond measure he sat down beside her. He cared not to speak, although the apparition laughed merrily, touched him lightly on the arm and sprang to her feet with "Light your cigar?", and like a fairy, a sylph gliding noiselessly across the room, she disappeared in the hallway that led to the kitchen. He heard a few hasty words spoken in a language he could not comprehend, and in an instant she returned with a burning match, which she applied to his cigar. He noticed the white fingers, the neatly trimmed nails, and on the index finger he saw a gold ring and an intricately woven chain bracelet of gold and silver linked alternately - a striking combination. She threw the burning match to the floor when the cigar was lighted, and both watched in silence the last spark as it burned brighter and suddenly went out.

He felt her warm breath upon his cheek, he touched her tapering fingers, cold as ice. She laughed and murmured something soft and low that he could not catch. He glanced quickly at her; she laid her delicate fingers on his arm, and in a sweet voice asked him the time. He reached for his watch, and at the same time the light was in some mysterious manner extinguished. He held the watch in front of his face, and in the impenetrable darkness he could not see its hands before his face. Radiant in her loveliness, he could see the lady plainly. She rose to her feet, her face wreathed in bewitching smiles, and everything in the room invisible in the Cimmerian veil except the rapturous figure. A terrible thought flashed through his mind. The very roots of his hair were freezing, and with a shriek on his lips he arose to his feet, while the form of the woman became fainter and fainter, and finally vanished into air as he fell unconscious to the floor.

When the gentleman came to, the sun was shining brightly in the room and the landlady was bending over him. At her instigation he rose wearily to his feet, and accepted her invitation to breakfast, but kept quiet the event of the previous night, and explained to her that he fell asleep on the settee, and probably sank to the floor. Lighting a cigar he strolled out in the yard, and finally sought his room. As he opened the door he noticed that his bed had been occupied, and the sheets were yet warm. He would seek the lady of the house and demand an explanation. He turned and looked again, rubbed his eyes. Was he dreaming? The bed quilts were neatly tucked, and there was nothing that would ever prove  that the bed had been occupied. Pshaw! His mind was wandering, the events of the night were playing upon his mind and he went down town. He sought a friend, a cool, resolute man to whom he imparted his story, and they agreed to watch together that night. His friend, Arthur Harrington, agreed to meet him at 10 o'clock and he repaired to a gunsmith and purchased a revolver and a dark lantern.

That night, in company with Harrington, he returned to his quarters at 10:15 o'clock and stepped into the parlor. The night was cloudy and rather dark, and with the light extinguished the two men awaited developments in silence.

The cathedral clock in the library chimed the eleventh hour, the quarter hour, the half hour, and then again the quarter hour. Now quiet. The silence reigned supreme. A shadowy figure appeared in the darkness. Harrington touched his friend on the arm. A stealthy tip-toeing in the hallway, the door moved slowly and an

instant later a tall, white figure of a man dressed in the fashion of by-gone ages, entirely out of proportion, glided, not walked, but moved mysteriously across the room and silently disappeared. A flash from the dark lantern. The hall door was still ajar. The two men stole into the corridor, when low voices were heard in the attic. Up the stairs they crept, Harrington leading the way. At the first landing they paused a moment, and in the light of the lantern, Harrington examined his revolver and muttered: "I'll make it a sorry night for any ghost prowling around the premises."

Again in darkness the two men with rapid pulses felt their way up the attic stairs, and when the head had been reached, Harrington quietly pushed in the door. On the opposite side of the room was a low bed, and in it lay an old man. Harrington guarded the door, while his friend crossed the room and pulled off the covers. Horrors! A skeleton lay there, exposed to full view by the bright bulls-eye lamp. A chuckle at the door, and a white form passed down the stairs. The two men sprang after the retreating form and ghost and pursuers rushed pell-mell down the stairs into the parlor, where Harrington dropped the lantern. The specter turned, and a hollow, mocking laugh was heard. Harrington fired a shot, the bullet in its flight, striking the apparition in the left side over the heart. A small stream like fire bled, and with the laugh dying on it's pale lips, the form faded away. A blue light was seen in the narrow hallway, and a moment later the woman of the night before appeared and placed the lamp on the table. "Good morning stranger", she uttered, the same remark she used the previous night.

Harrington was amazed at her fresh beauty, but determined to solve the mystery, he asked: "Where did you come from? Who is in the cellar?"

The lady smiled sweetly and nodded her head pleasantly, but did not deign to reply. Harrington essayed to seize her arm. Ugh! He grasped empty air. A moment later a cold hand settled on his forehead; a man of massive build entered from the kitchen, and having a revolver, fired at the woman, who fell to the floor with a shriek. Harrington returned the fire and bounded toward him, the light went out, and a moment later he stumbled over the open trap-door into the cellarway, where he was struck several sharp blows. His friend fared worse. His clothes were nearly torn off his body, and while he lay almost unconscious he heard two moans and cries of pain issuing from the cellarway in which Harrington had fallen. The spring in the clock broke, and all the china in the pantry was shaking violently. The very beams of the house were trembling, and it seemed as though all the elements were concentrating their furies on the place and wreaking vengeance of dread and dire. In the sitting room he saw for the third time the young woman in semi-deshibille this time, and a moment later a fair-looking man entered and fired a shot, which sent her shrieking to the floor.

When morning came the landlady again woke him from his deep sleep. He sought Harrington who was still unconscious in the cellar. A physician was summoned and he was resuscitated. The events of the past two nights were briefly narrated to the housekeeper who smiled faintly and said, "Yes, they say the house is haunted, and every night a young woman treads the carpet of this room. That is her picture over the mantlepiece. She was shot in the sitting room by her husband one afternoon several years ago. Her name was Stella, poor child. She was my only daughter."

The house still stands, though it has been remodeled and fitted up, and to this day strange sounds are heard after nightfall. Doors open and shut, and the floors creak mysteriously, and whenever a storm is raging, unearthly groans proceed from different parts of the house. It is needless to add that the gentleman never returned to his room.

March 31, 1889

Reprinted with the permission of the Rocky Mountain News.

1. The Albany Hotel, 17th and Stout St. Built in 1885, the Albany was said to be "The most elegantly furnished hotel between two oceans". Designed by local architect E. P. Brink, it had 155 rooms and 50 private baths. It was also the first hotel in the city to have electric lights.
Guests over the years included: William (Buffalo Bill) Cody, Annie Oakley, General and Mrs. Tom Thumb (famous P.T. Barnum midgets) and "16 comely daughters of Brigham Young".
A Denver landmark for over 91 years, the Albany was torn down in 1976 to make way for an office-hotel complex.

GHOULS THAT LABOR

Phantom Forms
That Flit Mysteriously Around the Scenes of Their Former Crimes.
A Corps of Disembodied Gravediggers
Haunt the Location of a Long Forgotten Cemetery.
Grave Desecrating
During their Lives Punished By an Eternal Repetition of the Ghastly Deed.

Four nights last week, commencing with Monday and concluding Thursday, mysterious transactions have taken place on one of the principal business streets in the heart of the city, that have caused the friends of a prominent man to inquire into his sanity, and even caused Chief Farley[1] to, for a moment, doubt the word of two of his most trusted officers. To those who retire before the hour of midnight, the story of the singular occurrence will read like a wild fiction, but it can be substantiated by those who toil while the city slumbers who stand ready to testify.

Passing the corner of Seventeenth and Arapahoe street in daylight no one would ever dream that for four consecutive nights seven strange forms have moved hither and thither in the full glare of the electric lights and have performed manual work. A gentleman, who lives on Logan Avenue near Sixteenth Street, was entertaining a party of friends at the Windsor[2] Monday night and of course, as is the custom on such occasions, he drank more than his usual quantity, and it was 12 o'clock before he started home. Seventeenth Street being his nearest route, he turned and walked up on the left side of the street. All absorbed in the meaning meant to be conveyed in a confidential chat bearing upon the election, he suddenly noticed a red light at his feet. In

fact, he had overturned a lantern. He glanced up and in front of him saw an excavation in the center of Arapahoe Street, commencing at the crossing and ending at the car track on Seventeenth Street, about four feet deep and two feet in width. While six men near busily engaged in throwing out the loose sand, the foreman stood beside the trench. He was compelled to walk around the pile of dirt, and continued his way up Seventeenth Street.

The event made an impression on his mind, and when he came down town at 7 o'clock in the morning, he looked out of the car window, rubbed his eyes, looked again, and reaching for the bell cord stopped the car. He walked over to the point where the trench was dug and could not even see a sign of work having been done there. He spoke to a man sweeping the dust out of the curves in the car tracks and received only a stare for a reply. When he informed his friends, they laughed suggestively.

That evening he was in a downtown saloon, and while talking the affair over, concluded he would go home, and as he passed the same corner he saw the identical men digging at the intersection of the streets, and to the end that no mistake should be made this time, he looked down into the hole. It was excavated fully five feet and the men, who were evidently Italians, were digging it deeper and deeper. He smiled to himself the following morning as he approached the corner, but on stepping off the car, was astonished not to see the earth piled up beside the track. Not the slightest evidence that the earth had been disturbed was visible and he walked to his office on Lawrence Street in a dazed condition.

Wednesday night he returned home and saw the men digging what looked as though it might be intended for a grave, and in a puzzled, perplexed frame of mind he went home and rolled and tumbled in his bed, only to find the street in the same condition Thursday morning as he had on the three preceding days. That night he resolved to watch. In company with a friend he passed the corner at 11:30. Not a soul could be seen. It was 11:58 when they returned. All they could see was a Broadway car, the last in, tearing down the street, and as it passed seven men walked out of the shadows on Arapahoe Street and approaching the corner, threw down their picks and shovels. Not a word was spoken, not a sign made, and under the slouch hats, pulled well down on their foreheads it was impossible to see their eyes.

From whence came these men and what their mission? Each seemed to know his place and each performed a pre-arranged function. There was a foreman, but he  directed them in nothing. A small box was suddenly, by some legerdemain, presented and the men fell to work. Commencing at the out-car track at the corner on the left hand side of Seventeenth Street looking toward the depot, they dug a trench across Seventeenth to the crossing in front of the Clifton House[3.], a man between each track and three men to the right, while the foreman paced around, a silent sentry. No man spoke. Where one mind acts in unison with another and men work in conjunction, words are meaningless and hence not used. No language could tell them more explicitly how to act than the magnetic manner, the mute method they had of exchanging their opinions. They dug deeper, down six feet, and still going deeper. The man, who had seen the apparition before, walked out to the track and spoke to the foreman; and he (it) turned a pair of dark eyes toward him and walked away.

"Here, come there, get out your lights." Both watchers started. It was the voice of one of the two policemen who hurried up.

"Stick up your red lights there! Suppose there was a fire and an apparatus came tumbling down the street, and into this hole. Get 'em out and no funny business about it."

Without a word, and with evident reluctance the red lanterns were taken out of the box and a match applied to the wicks by the police. Four men saw the seven.

It was then 4 o'clock in the morning. The officers lurked about the neighborhood until nearly 5 o'clock to see that the ordinance regarding lamps was not disregarded, and before going home the gentlemen who watched the men asked one of the officers how long it would take them to cover it.

"To complete the hole, take out the timber under the tracks and cover it...four hours."

The sound of the sergeant's whistle announced the hour of 5, and all went home, leaving the men at work.

When Chief Farley passed the same corner at 7 o'clock that morning on his way to headquarters , he met one of his detectives and stopped to talk a few moments, and while there marked the peculiar actions of a man who was gazing intently at the street and who acted as though he was intoxicated. As he passed the chief his cheek was pale, his lips quivered, his eyes were wild with excitement. The chief looked at the road and seeing nothing, walked away. Ten minutes later in the station he read the following report from one of his officers:

"Excavation twenty feet long, two wide and eight deep, seven men working, Seventeenth and Arapahoe. No red lights. Lights placed at 4 o'clock a.m."

The chief had just come from that corner and saw nothing of the sort. He called the officer in question, who was trying a case in the police court and asked him.

"Did you write this as a joke?"

"No sir, fact."

"Positive?"

"Yes, sir."

"Witness?"

"Yes, sir."

Policemen use no unnecessary words and speak shortly. He called the officer with him at the time to prove it.

"Come with me, gentlemen," said the chief. Seated in the pony patrol, they drove to the corner. Not the remotest evidence that the pick had ever been struck in the street was seen. Non-plussed the police could but say, "It was here at 5 o'clock."

An hour later the gentlemen reported the matter to the chief. He spoke of the two officers and was mystified beyond measure. Farley instructed the night sergeant to keep particular watch of that corner.

A curious thing in connection with the affair is that the men dug in the same spot, the second time and each time they dug tremendous holes, and have been seen at work up to within twenty minutes of daylight. The question now is, where do they go? Why do they dig? And how do they manage to cover up the evidence of their work? No one ever saw them put the trenches to practical use, and four men are prepared to swear they have seen the streets torn up four consecutive nights last week, and thousands of people who have crossed that place during the day can swear that they have not noticed it, have not seen it, and will probably not credit it. But the report lays in Chief Farley's office. The policeman saw with his own eyes, he spoke but was not answered, though his order was obeyed. A watch was kept Friday night, but the apparition failed to materialize.

The gentleman referred to is now in bed, confined by a raging fever brought on by the mental strain. Chief Farley is unable to explain, and the more it is investigated, the more mysterious it becomes. Every step the detectives take seem to lead them further away from the main facts of the case.

October 14, 1889

Reprinted with the permission of the Rocky Mountain News.

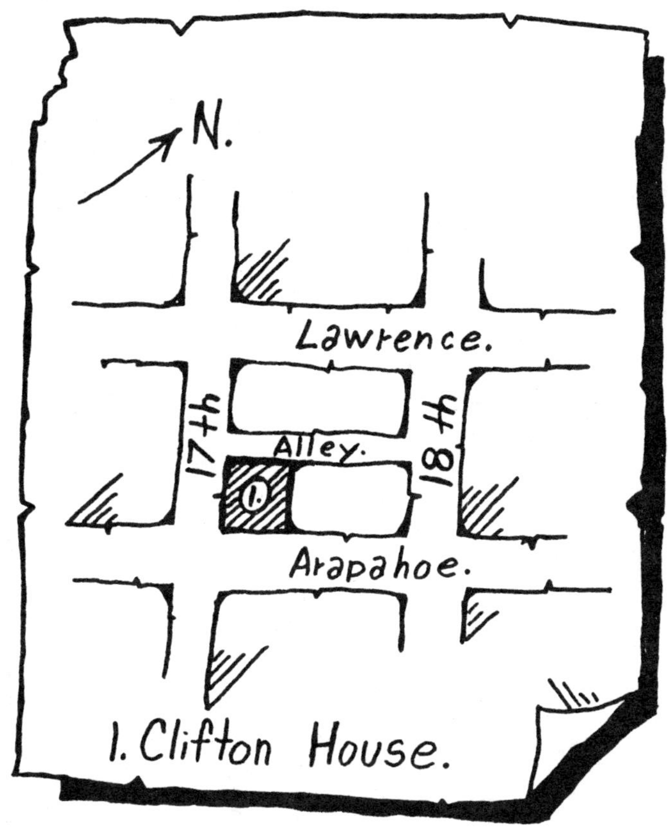

1. John f. Farley: Noted pioneer and Indian fighter. Denver Chief of police from 1889-1891.

2. Windsor Hotel, 18th and Larimer St: Opened in 1882, the Windsor cost over one million dollars to build. It was best remembered for its beautiful furnishings and interiors, including its opulent ballroom. Guests over the years included four U.S. Presidents, Marie Dressler and Oscar Wilde. Horace Tabor died there and Calamity Jane shot holes in the ceiling of the downstairs bar. The Windsor was also said to have a ghost or two of its own. A ghostly old man was seen sitting at the bar on occasion and a veiled woman roamed the hallways at night.

The Windsor was torn down in 1959 to make room for a larger hotel complex.

3. Clifton House, 17th and Arapahoe St. was built in 1867 by Henry Reitze and was one of Denver's first business blocks. In earlier times, it was used as a stopover for freighters en route to the mining camps with supplies. Torn down in 1924, the site is now part of the Denver National Bank Plaza.

FROM SHADOW'S VALE

Inexplicable Letter
Received from the Misty Realms Beyond the Grave.
An Old Resident of Denver
Recognizes the Handwriting of His Beloved Dead Daughter.
No Room for Doubt
That the Missive Came from One Who Had Passed Forever from Earth.

"A NEWS reporter?"

"Keerect."

"I knew it, although I haven't seen you for well nigh two years. My memory is wonderful sir."

The speaker was a man of some 70 summers, considerably bent in stature, and evidently the victim of some internal malady of a painful nature. His clothes, though somewhat worn, still bore indication of having been made "to order" and of first-class material. It was, however, the bright expression of the old man's features, especially his piercing sharp eyes, that the stranger was most impressed with.

"If you are not too busy, sir," he continued, "I would take it as a great favor if you will come with me to my home, where, if you are fond of a mystery, I can treat you to something that will set you thinking and possibly to writing also."

"A ghost story?"

"Well, not exactly, but something very closely approaching one."

Half an hour later the NEWS man was seated in a cozy little parlor on Welton Street, awaiting the old man and half expecting that an apparition would present itself in the darkness ere he had secured company.

"Think I had forgotten you?" the old man said apologetically on re-entering the room. "It was this letter that kept me so long. Someone must have been reading it unknown to me and failed to return it to the place in which I had it hidden. However, I found it at last, and now for my story."

"It is just three weeks ago today since I suffered the greatest calamity that has happened to me....the death of my daughter, Louise. She was the joy of my old age, and as good a girl as ever lived. But the fever is no respecter of an old man's feelings and my darling was carried off."

"To live with the angels," ventured the reporter.

"Ah! That's just what's troubling me," he replied. "I have been a Christian all my life, but I fear I am beginning to lose faith, and all on account of this letter. I hope you will refrain from passing judgement until I have told you all, for I know you must be incredulous when I say that the letter is nothing but a message from the other world, and sent to me without the agency of medium or any so-called spiritual agency. You see the texture of the paper is of a flimsy nature and entirely different from anything you ever saw; the envelope the same; but the writing, there can be no mistake about; it is that of my poor daughter, written certainly with a peculiar kind of blood-red ink, but beyond doubt her own writing.

Now, I want you to observe the date on the message as well as the day on which it came through the mail just eight days ago and nearly two weeks after Louise's lifeless body was laid in Riverside Cemetery. Of course it is a most mysterious affair, but I cannot get it out of my mind, more especially as one night when she and I were discussing "the hereafter", so to speak, she told me in the most serious terms that if she should die before me she would send me a message, provided it were possible. The girl certainly never would have deceived me by writing this letter before she died. And as to the penmanship, why I would swear to it being hers. Here, I have some letters written by her when alive. Just glance through them and judge for yourself."

They were certainly very much alike and as the writing was rather straggling and uncommon it seemed all the more remarkable that the same formation of the letters had been adhered to in each epistle.

"There is a marked similitude", replied the NEWS man, "but had your daughter no sister or near friend who could imitate her writing?"

"No, she was my only child and among her acquaintances I know of no one who wrote exactly like her or who, much less would have played a practical joke of such a ghastly nature on her sorrowing father."

Here certainly was a mystery, and like most trans-mundane affairs, "past finding out". Had someone at last sent tidings across the dread line that separates man from the life beyond?

"Can you offer an explanation of this yourself, sir?" queried the scribe as he looked enquiringly into the old man's face.

The poor fellow was now trembling with emotion. "Explanation; no, I have none to offer. Would that it had never happened."

It was not without a considerable feeling of curiosity that the reporter perused the "uncanny" document , whilst his companion, it may be, awaited some feasible solution of the difficulty from the newspaper man. The letter was not long and read as follows:

"My Dear Father - Ever since I passed away from earth I have been longing to fulfil my promise to you, and let you know how it fares with the souls that have left their bodies, and more especially my own position from a spiritual point of view. Oh! I am happy, so happy and it is all so natural that I should be just where I am. It seems as if it had all been pre-arranged and could not be otherwise, just like the flower blooms at its appointed time. It will surprise you that I am still in the earthly atmosphere, which I seem to gaze on with far different eyes and to see new glories on every side. Everything is changing and instinct tells me that I must proceed with the stream, where I know not, and have no fear as I feel that I am in the pure waters of life and in the end, or rather through the centuries that will never end, my bark is safe here. Here only is happiness, and you, dear father, will soon be enjoying it, not with me, for earthly ties and affections are as nothing compared with the joys that are assured to those who have secured an eternity of bliss. Of the devil I know nothing. On earth I never did believe in the old-fashioned fellow, and I feel all the more certain that if he does exist it is in the beautiful nature that, in the end, rights everything that is wrong, over-coming evil with good. Never before has the liberty been afforded to a spirit to communicate in an earthly, tangible way with a human being. Why I have been chosen for the office I know not. It may be that a new era for the intelligent guidance of the people is about to open up. Would that it will be so."

LOUISE

Having finished reading the message, both men sat for a full minute staring intently into each others face as it were to find some clue to the mystery. To the NEWS man it now seemed possible to explain most anything - even to the politics of N.P. Hill[1]...but here in western parlance was a "corker", a regular rip snorter that would puzzle a Philadelphia lawyer.

"Well, what do you think of it?" asked the old man breaking the silence.

"Think of it. I consider it one of the most remarkable and sensible epistles that have ever emanated from spirit land and I will take the liberty of laying the whole thing before the public discussion. As to my own opinion about the genuineness of the document - well....."

"Oh, there can be no mistake about that - there is my daughter's own hand-writing. It could not possibly be a forgery."

The words now suggested to the reporter the question, was the old man altogether "genuine" himself, but a look into his pale, earnest face dispelled all suspicion of that kind. Then he was drawn into a conversation on general topics, with the view of testing that he had seldom conversed with a brighter intellect or a more level-headed man of his years.

And so the mystery remains unfathomed. It may arouse an inquiry among folks of a supernatural turn of mind and may be eventually explained. The letter is open to inspection by all and the father of the dead girl will facilitate any examination, as to the young woman's death and burial or any other matter of importance. The occurrence is certainly without parallel, even in the annals of spirit land, and should furnish much food for reflection.

September 29, 1890

Reprinted with the permission of the Rocky Mountain News.

1. Nathaniel P. Hill (1932 - 1900). Famed Colorado Senator who was best remembered for building the first smelting plant in the state (1868). He was also, at one time or another, President of the Florence Oil Co., Mayor of Black Hawk, a professor at the School of Mines and proprietor of the Denver Republican.

TRAILING A SPECTER

Consternation Produced
in Different Telegraph Offices by the Appearance of a Mystic Message. No
Trace of the Sender Found
Operators Puzzled by a Nightly Recurrence.
Two Intrepid Employees
Undertake to Find the Wire Tapper and are Successful.

For the past two weeks, one of the telegraph companies here has experienced a great deal of difficulty with one of its southern routes. The story, as told by one of the operators, is a peculiar one.

Every office has a call, that is, Denver is known as D, Boulder as G, Colorado Springs as CG. About two weeks ago, Denver was called from an office which signed AZ. Now, there is no such office in the state, hence the case becomes a mystery. The chief operator went to the key and asked the strange office to give its full name. This he refused to do until they were ready to receive his message, claiming that his was a relaying or repeating office, and that he was sending matter from "K.S." or Kansas City.

The case was a strange one, and he was told to go ahead. A message was sent, but no such party as the one addressed lived in this city. As the message was sent collect, an investigation was instituted, and when Kansas City checked back it was found that no such matter was ever sent from that office.

The mystery deepened.

Nearly every night the office called Denver, but the persons to whom the dispatches were sent could never be found.

The case was a desperate one.

Last week the following message, marked "rush", was sent:

Translated in English this reads: I .grave was my a in man easy who rest in not my will time I on deciphered earth, is drank message considerable this and Until one .divide night or was ridgeway killed continental on the what as is known is as what the on continental killed ridgeway was or night divide. one Until and this considerable, message drank is earth deciphered on I time will my not in rest who easy man in a my was grave. I

Llaksah dr

Now, this message was meaningless, and though the entire force of the office was put to work upon it, it could not be worked out. It was something they could not understand. "A.Z." office certainly possessed a fast sender, who signed "K.X." a most peculiar signature. "K.X." never opened his key on Denver, while no one in town could take matter as fast as he rushed it in. He roasted them frightfully. No one could read his mysterious message, and one night he asked if they could not take it to one of the cable clerks. It was done.

It was of no use.

Finally "A.Z." began to send "1,3," "1,3" forward, backward, either way, O.K. Ah!

The night chief grasped the message and this is the way he read it. Following what he thought were the instructions, he tackled the message, reading the first and third, fifth and seventh words, and so on, which made the dispatch read like this:

I was a man who in my time on earth drank considerable, and one night was killed on what is known as the continental ridgeway or divide. Until this message is deciphered I will not rest easy in my grave. R.D. Haskall

A Ghost! A spirit on the wire!

A spectral operator!

Cold chills chased one another down the backbone of those present. Beads of sweat stood on the brow of each.

With nervous hand and faint of heart, the night chief operator opened his key and said: "Don't 13" (Don't understand.)

Quick as a flash, the sounder rattled back the following, in the best quality of Morse they had ever heard:

"I was a telegrapher who at one time worked in New York State, and in 1848-49 caught the gold fever, and came West. As I said, I drank considerably and, one night, in a drunken brawl I was killed on the old Pueblo trail, a few miles from what is now Palmer Lake[1], on the Continental Divide. My spirit has roamed about and until I make known the cause of my death, I cannot rest in my grave. The telegraph pole from which I am sending this is planted directly over my grave, the butt of the pole resting on my breast. I will call you up regularly for three nights, and if I raise you, answer. My message reads backward the same as forward.   H."

A couple of the operators laughed at this, and the sounder clicked heavily, "Ha, Ha," and they heard the circuit close.

The two operators swore that someone was fooling them, and they volunteered to search for the date over the spook's grave.

Two days later found them walking over the road the other side of Palmer Lake. As they rounded a small hill or divide, one of them who had been counting the poles, remarked that they were fifteen miles from the lake, and they sat down to await developments. They did not wait long, for in a few moments they felt a strange feeling creep over them, and then transfixed, they saw something that they are not likely to forget.

From the bottom of the pole they were watching, they noticed a dim, blue light. A white vapor arose, which gradually took form, and in a few moments had assumed the shape of a man in white, holding in his right hand a telegraph key.

When he reached the top of the pole he quickly cut the wires and began to telegraph something, and in a few minutes he slid down the pole and disappeared.

When the operators returned to Denver, they found the following message that the operator had sent:

"Your two investigators here. They have seen me. Farewell to earth. I have been heard and seen. I am satisfied. Good-bye.   H."

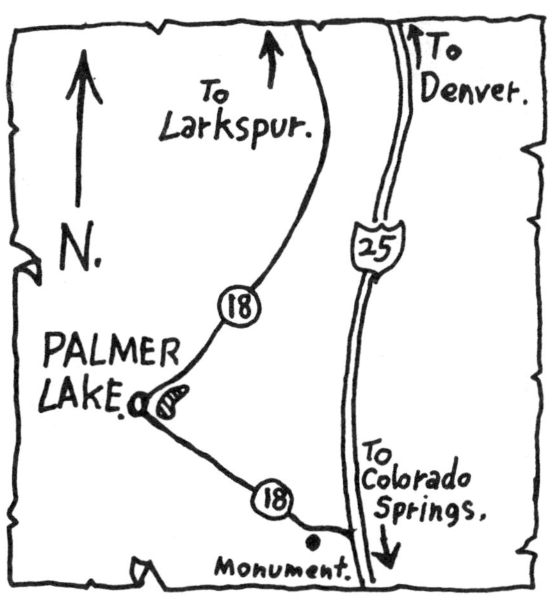

March 9, 1891

Reprinted with the permission of the Rocky Mountain News.

1. Palmer Lake: A popular turn-of-the-century resort, 40 miles south of Denver and 20 miles north of Colorado Springs.

A GHOST STORY

The early placer miners who occupied Georgia Gulch, west of Gray's Peak,[1] were often scared by a great apparition. In those days Georgia gulch was surrounded by a thick pinon forest, which for years was known as "The Devil's Den". It was in fact, a wild, dreary place and many strange tales have been told about the horrible beasts that inhabited it. The little stream, Cicero creek, runs though the gulch and at one time it was reported that a horrible dragon with wings of terrible length and eyes as large as dinner plates and a mouth full of appalling teeth, inhabited the Den.

It is said that this dragon's body was covered with large scales and when it flew from one part of the forest to the other, the noise of its wings could be heard for miles and sounded like the approach of some terrific storm.

A miner named Carroll passed through the outer edge of the woods one evening near sundown when he was startled by a tempestuous noise. A sickening smell seemed to fill the air. Looking up, he saw this terrible animal sail through the air in the direction of some cattle feeding on the range just outside Georgia gulch.

Suddenly, it dashed downward and arose again almost instantly with a cow in its gigantic claws. It flew in the direction of the Grand [2] and with a splash, disappeared beneath the water.

Carroll stood almost paralyzed and in telling the story afterwards to a crowd of loafers in the camp store, he stated that the water in the river foamed and boiled for more than twenty minutes. A party of ten was made up to either capture or kill the beast and for days they hunted the forest but did not see anything of the animal. This was long before the jag cure establishments were dreamed of and we never heard what became of poor Carroll.

March 19, 1892
Field and Farm - Denver, Co.

1. Gray's Peak - Ninth highest peak in Colorado (14,270 ft.)
   Named for Dr. Asa Gray; 19th century botanist.
2. Probably refers to Grand Lake. (See map)

WORK OF A GHOST

A Mystery
About the Gunnison Jail That Makes a Man's Flesh Creep.
Spooks Float in the Prison
and Liberate the Prisoners in Broad Daylight.
No Means Found for Keeping the Supernatural Visitor Out of the Place.

Special to the News:

GUNNISON, CO, MAY 18 - The prisoners confined in the county jail escaped this afternoon while the sheriff and his deputies were attending a circus. There were three prisoners in the jail; Tom Burns, who killed a man in Lake City a month ago, a man named Asktin, who was arrested at Creede for forgery, and an insane prisoner from Baldwin. The first two are prisoners of Hinsdale county and were brought to Gunnison and lodged in jail here for safekeeping.

A mystery surrounds the jail break, which the sheriff and his party are unable to unravel. About 2 weeks ago, when Sheriff Deering came into the corridor of the jail, he found the two huge iron bolts on the cell, in which Burns, the Lake City murderer was confined, thrown back and there was nothing to prevent the prisoner from going into the corridor. The sheriff knew positively that he had slipped the bolts into the sockets the night before, as was his usual custom and he questioned Burns concerning the matter.

Burns said that during the night a phantom appeared, who had his throat cut from ear to ear, stalked about the cell and disappeared though the door. The prisoner himself could not have done it, as he could not reach the bolts from the inside of his cell. The iron work is so close that the spaces between it are not over two inches square, and it is impossible for anyone on the inside to get his hand through. Besides, it requires all the strength of a man with both hands who is on the outside to move the bolts.

None of the other prisoners could have opened it, as they were securely locked in their cages.

The following evening, Sheriff Deering took particular pains in locking up the three prisoners, but the next morning the cage was open again.

The sheriff says he is not superstitious, but he could not help thinking there was something supernatural and miraculous about this. During the day, he carefully examined the cell and every corner of the jail and also the prisoners, thinking they might have some instruments with which the bolts might be thrown back, but nothing was found.

The sheriff was determined to baffle the efforts of the spook and made some hard wood pins, which he put in such a position that the bolts could not be moved while the pins were there and they could not be reached from the inside.

The pins did no good, for the next morning the bolts were back as usual.

Today, before going to the circus, the sheriff locked his prisoners in their cells and upon returning, he found the door leading to the corridor of the jail battered and the lock destroyed, the door being open.

An examination of the cages disclosed that they were unlocked and the bolts drawn and the prisoners from Hindsdale county were gone. The insane prisoner sat in a chair, but no information could be gained from him. It is evident that the prisoners had help from the outside. Men are scouring the country in every direction and the sheriff hopes to recapture the prisoners.

May 5, 1892

Reprinted with permission of the Rocky Mountain News.

A TEN-MILE GHOST

Ten-Mile Ghost
Drives a Man Out of House and Home.
The Spook Baffles Description and Eludes Capture.

From the Leadville Chronicle:

Mr. John Hargan, a man who has heretofore been credited with an unusual amount of hard common sense has been driven out of his house at Recene,[1.] by a series of circumstances which have plunged that little town into a fever of superstitious awe and excitement. In order to fully understand the case that is at present agitating the denizens of Ten-Mile, it becomes necessary to go somewhat into the past. The Hargan family, which consists of Mr. and Mrs. Hargan and two children occupied *a little house* close to the foot of Ten-Mile Avenue, or rather what was Ten-Mile Avenue before the devastating breath of the recent fire (1881) swept over it and across the avenue tracks. Living with the family temporarily was a prospector whom Mr. Hargan was grubstaking. These are the dominate persons of the affair.

The house consisted of four rooms, the two middle ones being used as sleeping apartments and one occupied by the Hargans and other by the prospector.

About two weeks ago the first of a chain of *remarkable manifestations* took place.

The family was, one evening, seated in the front room when one of the little children sprang up and cried out, "*Who is that looking in the window?*" and ran tremblingly to her mother's side. At the same instant there was a loud knock on the

glass. Hargan and his friend, both ran to the door and threw it open. The moon was shining quite brightly outside and no one in sight anywhere........... nothing but a broad expanse of freshly fallen snow, untracked within *a hundred feet* of the house.

Puzzled and alarmed, they returned and questioned the child. All she knew was that a man with a very white face had been looking in through the window and when she screamed, he suddenly disappeared. Mr. Hargan, who is not troubled with any superstitious fancies, tried to laugh off the matter and attributed the ghostly visitation simply to some hungry tramp attracted by the warmth and light within.

An hour or two passed and matter was well nigh forgotten, when the family was *thrown into consternation* by a second rap, however, and sharper than before. Again a rush was made for the door and again nothing save the untrodden

untrodden snow greeted their eyes. By this time, thoroughly alarmed, Mr. Hargan took a seat close to the window and within a foot or two of the door and patiently waited. In the course of twenty minutes there were two loud raps at the door, but their echo had scarcely died away when Hargan was on the threshold. There was not a trace of anyone outside and ***complete-ly unnerved,*** he re-entered the room and turned the lock. There were no other manifestations that evening, nor the next, but the day after that, at about noon, while Mrs. Hargan was engaged at some household work, there were three or four impatient raps at one of the middle doors of the house. She turned to it, supposing it to be some of the neighbors when the door was suddenly pushed open in her face. No one was there, the room was absolutely empty and half-fainting with fright, she ran to get ***her husband.*** Ever since that time these manifestations have continued and scarcely an evening passed that the raps were not heard on the doors or windows.

The most startling of them, however, have taken place within the past few days. One night, in the latter part of the week, the prospector, who was quietly sleeping in the center room, was awakened by feeling something jump upon his feet and crouch there. His mind filled with the uncanny events of the two weeks past, and he did ***not dare to move*** and scarcely breathing, lay quite still. An instant later, the thing upon the bed crowded toward him and he felt the clutch of a hand upon his shoulder. He had pulled the cover up over his head, but could stand it no longer and gave a loud, long shriek of terror. The sound broke the spell and he felt his body instantly relieved of the weight, as at the same moment Hargan rushed, revolver in hand, into the room.

The story was told in a few words and they hastily decided to ***say nothing*** about it to Mrs. Hargan, who was in a pitiable state of nervous prostration. Next night, the husband made some excuse to sleep with the prospector and with his revolver in convenient reach, they retired. Late at night, when everything was enveloped in pitchy darkness, Hargan was awakened by someone passing their hands over his side. His first impulse was to reach for his gun, but an uncontrollable terror seized him and he was unable to move. Half fainting, he felt something creep over him and then jump ***to the floor*** with an audible concussion. For an instant he lay mute and motionless, and then was aroused by the screams of his wife. The room in which she slept had a window opening to the old town of Kokomo[2] and when her husband rushed in, she said she had awakened to see the black profile of someone between this and her. As she stared at it, the head slowly turned and by a faint phosphorescent glow that surrounded it, she made out the figure of *a **man***. There, for the first time, she found her voice and as she cried out, the figure faded and disappeared.

This experience was sufficient and the family sat up during the remainder of the night. As soon as possible the next day, they moved out and since then the house has stood vacant and empty.

No one can be induced to even spend a night in it and the owner is anxious to give it rent free to any tenant who will brave its unknown terrors.

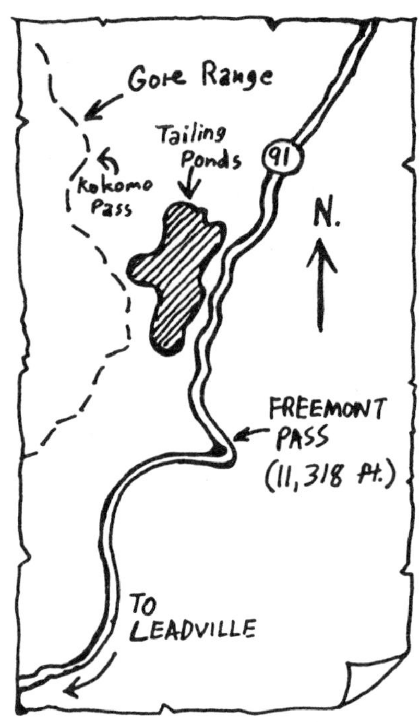

December 15, 1881

Reprinted with the permission of the Rocky Mountain News.

1. Recene - Mining town in Summit County on line of the Ten-Mile extension of the D & RG Railway. (Denver and Rio-Grande) Population 750; Altitude 10,500 feet. Distance; Leadville 20 miles (Northeast); Breckenridge 28; Robinson 2; Red Cliff 12. (Colorado State Directory, 1881)

2. Kokomo - Sister city of Recene, the two were separated by a single street. Once located near the foot of Freemont Pass, Kokomo along with Recene, have long since disappeared. Bought up in 1966 by the Climax Molybdenum Co., the town was abandoned and soon buried under a huge tailing pond.

A CRIME IN THE CAÑON

**An Old-Timer Railroader
Relates a Romance of Gore and Ghosts on the South Park Road.
A Ghost in Platte Canon
that Frightened a Stalwart Engineer and His Stalwart Fireman.
A Scene of Sepulchral Horror
Enacted Night after Night on the Lonely Rocks of the Gulch.**

"Do you believe in ghosts?" asked a well-known Denver engineer, who is also somewhat of a barnacle, to a NEWS reporter recently,.

"No." said the reporter, "Do you?"

"Well, kind of. You see, I've seen some strange things in my time. In the first place, I was kind of a juvenile barnacle."

"How's that?"

"Why, I wasn't the first kid born in the Cherry Creek settlement, or anything of the kind, but I was very much of a kid when I came here with my parents in a bull team; in fact I was only about five years old.

We had to rustle in those early days, I tell you, but there was a good deal of fun, too. I remember something about the old-time dances of those days, though I was quite a kid, you know, and then when I got to be a young man, I remember the starting of the old volunteer fire companies and all the fun of the 60's and 70's. It has always seemed to me though, that the fun was all when I was a mere kid and that there were no days like the pioneer days. You bet your life there was more social life in the 60's than there has been since. You see when everybody knew everybody else, there was more sport and more good feeling.

But I am getting way off from my story.

You see, back in the 70's when the Colorado Central was in its infancy, I went on a train for the first time braking. I am not much over 30 now, but I've seen lots of variety in the railroad business. Well, now I'll settle down to business.

'Twas not so many years ago that these things happened. I ain't much good on dates but it was not-so-many years ago that I was firing on the South Park, having left the Colorado Central after working my way up to fireman and then getting into a row with the engineer."

"I can't catch on to where the joke comes in." said the reporter, who was getting a little tired.

"Hold 'er down, young man, and I'll get to it. I presume like every other tenderfoot, you think the mountains are wonderful?"

"Yes, indeed," said the reporter, "and the South Park division between Denver and Como goes through some of the most picturesque and beautiful scenery in the world."

"You're right, young man. There ain't no such dandy scenery anywhere as there is on the South Park! Now, I am a little rough, I am. Colorado railroaders nowadays are just as high-toned as anybody, but I've been rustling a good deal ever since I was a kid and I ain't much on language or style. But if you'll stick close to the cab and hold on, I'll steer you right through. Now, I haven't got no fancy pull on these things, but I'll just ram her though in my own way. Now as you were saying, the Platte Canon is a dandy. I know how it strikes a tenderfoot, for I've heard 'em tell it many a time, to enter a canon, and I must say it is a glorious sight to go snorting into the gorges and see the big rocks on either side of you and the rich green grass, wherever grass can grow and the prospect of more rocks ahead. The Rio Grande's too much on rocks, but the South Park is just easy and pleasant with plenty of scenery and considerable variety. Did you think how Injuns would look on them rocks in that canon?"

"Yes," said the reporter, "I've thought of it a great many times."

"Well, there was Indians there once and there was miners traveling over the rocks when I was a kid. In fact, they used to travel everywhere in those days. I remember when I was running on the South Park, there was an old fellow, that is, he was old in looks, who lived in a little shanty near Webster. He was a rough sort of a cuss, but he had as pretty a wife and as pretty kids as you ever saw in your life. Now there was another fellow who lived down by Como, who was pizen against the old fellow. They quarreled over one thing and another and the fellow at Como, whose name was Smith, swore he'd kill the other fellow and burn down his cabin. The other fellow, whose name was Ike Taylor, paid mighty little attention to these threats, but the other cuss kept his word and one dark night while Taylor was over to Breckenridge, his cabin was burned down and the wife and three kids was burned to death."

"Did Smith set the fire?"

"I don't know, but I know when Taylor came back the next day, Smith skipped out mightily lively and fled into the canon. There was no railroad in them days, though one was built soon after. Smith seemed to be afraid to go to town for some reason or another and stayed up round the canon, but Taylor found out his hiding place, having started after him with a bowie knife and gun. People say they met in the canon and had a fight with knives. At any rate, the story didn't turn out well. Taylor's body was found in the gulch, all smashed up as if it had been thrown down from the rocks and it looked as if a knife had been stuck in it, though the coroner wasn't certain of it."

"What became of Smith?"

"As the poet remarks, 'that's one of the things what no feller can find out,' I expect there's so many Smiths in the world he's got lost in the general numerousness of the family, but now, I'll come to the ghost.

As I was telling you, some years after this, I was firing on the South Park. One night I was working on an engine and it was a pretty dark night, too. We had got past Dome Rock and was steering along pretty slow for Denver. We hadn't got many passengers, but was just bringing up some cars for an excursion train the next day. Suddenly, Jim Green, the engineer, looks up at me and he says, "Bill, I feel kind of funny."

"What's the matter?" said I, "Have you got the colic or the jim-jams, or are you simply bilious?"

"No." says Jim, "I don't drink and I haven't 'et nothing, but what's that light up there on the rocks?"

"Dog-goned if I know," Said I, looking straight up and seeing the light. "There ain't no fools setting the brush afire is there?"

"No." he says, "It don't look like that. Looks kind of weird, don't it, kind of blue like some of them scenes at Forester's opera house."

"My God!" says he, sudden like, "What's that? Didn't you see somebody jump down on to the track?"

"I saw something." says I. "I wonder if some d______d lunatic is trying to kill himself."

"Was that what it was?" asked the reporter, who was getting interested.

"No, I should say not. The figure what jumped or was throwed off was white, but we couldn't find nothing on the track or in the Platte in any direction."

"What was it?"

"Young man, may I be smashed up on a narrow gauge engine if I don't think it was a ghost."

"What makes you think so?"

"Why, bless your boots, we got ketched out again on the road a few nights afterwards and saw the same thing all over again. Only this time, there was two men on the rocks and they had a struggle there and one of them seemed to stab the other with a knife and then throw him over into the Platte. I run on the road two or three years and I saw the blamed thing every night I was out, always in the same place and look here, I'll be dog-goned if we didn't see something else.

One night on Kinosha hill we saw a cabin all on fire. It was at a coal pit. We first saw the cabin, then we heard a woman and some children scream, but we found out afterwards that there wan't no fire near Webster that night and there weren't no cabin in the place where we saw it, but we were told by some old-timers that this was where Taylor's cabin stood, and I believe 'em."

"Have you ever told this story to the Union Pacific people?"

"Yes, I used to tell it to Strahorn and I've told it to Henry James and to Egbert, but they told me I was either a cussed fool or a liar or words to that effect and they never would publish the story, for they thought it might hurt the road. Let's go and take a drink."

October 19, 1885

Reprinted with the permission of the Rocky Mountain News.

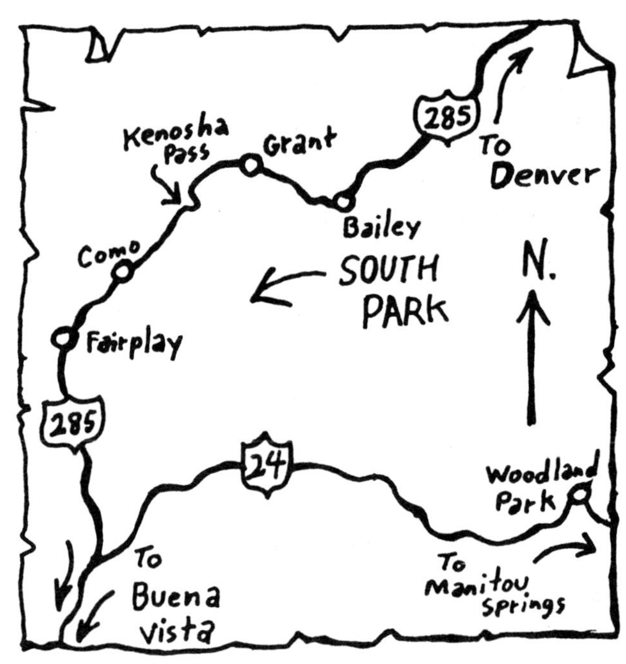

October 19, 1885

Reprinted with the permission of the Rocky Mountain News.

1. South Park - Southwest of Denver on Highway 285, through the town of Bailey, up the Platte Canyon and over 10,000 ft. Kenosha Pass. A large park-like area 3,500 square miles in diameter (roughly three times the size of Rhode Island), it is an average of 9000 ft. above sea level. The park is ringed by mountains; the Elkhorns to the East, the Mosquito range to the West and North and the Collegiates and Sangre de Cristos to the South.

THREE BRIGANDS FROM ROSITA

<h1 style="text-align:center">Lives and Deeds of a Gang
of Desperadoes in the Early Days of Colorado.
High Handed Manner
in Which They Carried Things for a While and Their Final Fate.
The Ghost of the Old Bridge.</h1>

Correspondence of the Tribune:

Rosita, August 25.--One would scarcely believe today that the quiet little village of Rosita[1], nestled among the green hills of Custer County, was once the scene of a bloody tragedy. In the upper part of the town, on the road leading to the Bassick mine, is a little bridge, spanning a wide ravine. Many curious stories are told by timid people, of ghosts seen flitting from beneath this structure on dark and dismal nights. A grim, tall man, with a bright saber, and with eyes like balls of fire, is seen walking the girders of this bridge in the dead of the night. Even the house dogs partake of the superstition--if it is such--for they bay at him from the hillsides, but dare not approach.

The cause of these wild apprehensions is a matter of history. In an early day some Germans discovered a rich mine a few rods above this bridge and in sight of the village. They called their mine the Pocahontas. Up to this time all had been peace and happiness in the little town. But the fame of the Pocahontas, with its rich deposits of gold and silver, soon attracted the greedy fortune seekers from all parts of the country and in a short time Rosita was a bustling camp. Hotels, stores and saloons went up like magic, and less than three months from the discovery of the wonderful Pocahontas, Rosita had a thousand or more population.

Among those who came was a trio of bold and daring villains. They were one W.A. Stewart, Colonel Boyd, and one Colonel Graham--the last as "mild a man as ever scuttled a ship or cut a throat."

Stewart and Boyd opened a bank and represented themselves to be capitalists, while Graham, their pal, fitted up and ran a saloon or ginmill.

Stewart, previous to settling in Rosita, had been a resident of Denver. He will be remembered by old citizens, as the man who, many years ago, built a fine cottage residence on Capitol Hill and fitted up an extensive winter garden and who, in a short time, became so popular with the people that his name was quite prominently mentioned in connection with the Mayoralty. In fact, the nomination was tendered him by one of the political parties.

Previously to settling in Denver, he had been known by another name than Stewart--had been one of the boldest and most successful robbers in America--or in England. He had robbed thirty different banks in America, in sums ranging from ten to a hundred thousand dollars each. After the most of his confederates had been captured and landed in the penitentiaries, Stewart became alarmed and emigrated to the West. Here, he joined a church, wore the plain habiliments of a gentleman and associated with none but the better classes.

For a time all went smoothly, yet he longed for his villainous associates. When the news came of the finding of the Pocahontas, he went to Rosita and there associated himself with two congenial spirits--Boyd and Graham.

Colonel Boyd, the second figure in this trio of villains, had once been Mayor of Baxter Springs, in Arkansas, had been proprietor of faro banks and dens of infamy and lastly had murdered a couple of men, and then, in disguise, had escaped to the West. He had no money but had the nerve. Stewart had both. So they embarked in business together.

Graham had been an officer in the Army during the rebellion, had been discharged and came West for adventure. He was a reckless gambler and soon was "broke". At Hugo, on the Kansas-Pacific railroad, he shot and robbed a paymaster of the Army and was wounded in return himself, but came immediately to Denver to squander, at cards, his ill-gotten gain. Here, he was arrested, tried for his crime of robbery and sent to the penitentiary at Canon City for a term of ten years. Soon after, he made his escape and got into the mountains of Custer County. A Sheriff and two deputies pursued him, came upon him unarmed and shot him down like a wild beast. He was returned to prison in his wounded condition and after much suffering, recovered.

An appeal was made to the Governor in his behalf and for his late suffering and in consideration of services rendered in the war, that official pardoned him. Graham went immediately to Rosita and opened a saloon for the ostensible purpose of immediate support and to enable him to murder the three men who had lately captured him. This, he openly avowed.

Stewart and Boyd took Graham into their ring and the three, on a dark and rainy night, with some hired ruffians, jumped the Pocahontas mine and held it by force of arms. The mine was considered worth half a million of money. For days, armed men, made mad by whiskey, marched in front of the mine and defied the people. The Sheriff was powerless. The Governor was appealed to, but before the Territorial militia could be got on the ground, the scene had changed. Graham had espied one of his victims on the street and shot him down where he stood, exclaiming: "There are two more. When they are dead, then my work is done." He then hid himself for a time in the Pocahontas mine and was protected from the populace by the drunken guard at the entrance.

Quietly the determined men of Rosita formed a vigilance committee and resolved to put an end to this reign of terror. Everything ready, they were proceeding to the mine to give battle to the armed mob in possession, when they espied the man Graham, with a pistol in either hand walk from his concealment and start toward the town. Hiding themselves behind a hill, they awaited until he arrived at the bridge (before spoken of) when a deadly fire was opened on him and he fell, pierced by a score of bullets. This struck terror to his fellows and the armed men at the mine threw down their guns and ran in all directions.

Boyd made his escape, but was pursued to Canon city and captured. He was returned to Rosita to be hung but was finally released on condition that he give up the keys to the bank safe in which was supposed to be considerable money deposited by the citizens and immediately leave the country, never to return. There was no money found in the safe. The late proprietors had already robbed it.

Stewart reached New York in safety, only to be identified by the detectives, who, for ten long years, had lost his trail. He was put upon trial, convicted and sentenced to a life term at Sing Sing. He is now making boots for the State of New York and paying the penalty of his crimes. Boyd went to Missouri and it is said, died a violent death at the hands of the James boys, who suspected him of treachery.

Thus would end the history and partially the memory of the Three Brigands of Rosita--were it not that the pallid ghost of the lean, lank Graham still haunts the little bridge near where he fell.

Fat Contributor.

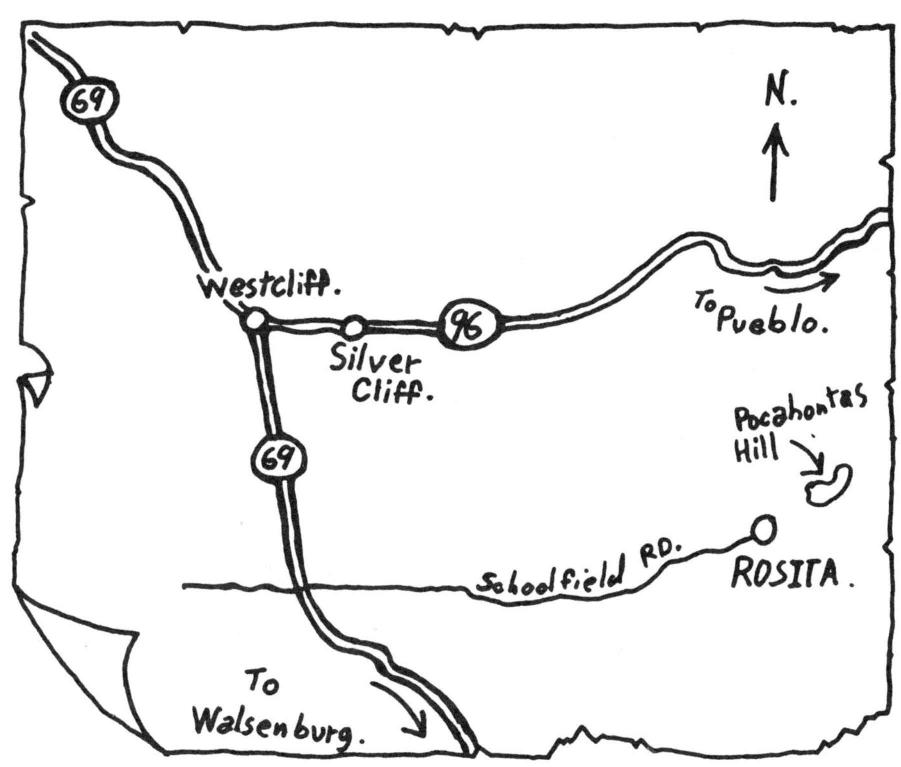

August 28, 1881
From the Denver Tribune
Colorado Historical Society

1. Rosita: Located 10 miles southeast of Westcliff in the Wet Mountain Valley, Rosita was once a thriving community. Founded in 1881, when silver was discovered in the nearby hills, it grew to a population of 1500 and was the original seat of Custer County. Several businesses were established there, including a bank, numerous hotels, a brewery and a newspaper (The Rosita Index). But, as is the case with some mining towns, the silver played out. By the turn of the century, Rosita began a long steady decline and was finally abandoned in 1978.

THE PHANTOM TRAIN

A Spectacle
that Made Brave Men Cowards and Drove the Weak Insane.
Chased by a Ghostly Train
Over the Backbone of the Great Continental Divide.
The Apparition
Which Haunted Grand Canon and Was Eventually Laid to Rest.

Mountain engineers are perhaps the most fearless class of men in the world. Journeys of so perilous a nature that the blood of an ordinary man would curdle at the bare thought of one undertaken are successfully made by them, and under circumstances of so trying a character that, on reflection, the average man would marvel at.

Those men who ride hundreds of miles through the mountains are seldom frightened, but today, there resides in Denver, a man who would not "pull" a train over Marshall Pass[1.] for a cool million, and when the name of the famous place is mentioned, he involuntarily clenches his hands and pales visibly.

Several years ago, there was a story circulated that three times a week, a phantom train went steaming over the pass and that ghostly forms could be seen through the car windows and although the statements in regard to it were incoherent, engineers began to regard a certain portion of the track with suspicion, usually hugging the rails there as close as possible.

One morning a freight "runner" pulled into Green River and informed the operator that he had seen the train and so earnestly did he plead with the master mechanic, that he was given an engine on the Salt Lake division. Other experiences were related and it became almost a weekly occurrence that some engineer would report having seen a train of which the dispatcher had no record and could not account for. In nearly every instance the engineers who complained were those who pulled the night passenger, which reached Green River at 7 o'clock in the morning. One engineer who had twice seen the much talked of train, pulled out of Salida as white as the snow on the ground and the following morning the fireman brought the engine into Green River, the brakeman firing, and the engineer in an insensible condition. He had seen the phantom train and that was his last trip on the road.

77

The regular train was then placed in the hands of an old and tried engineer, by the name of Nelson Edwards, who had as a fireman - Charles Whitehead. Both men were cool and calculating, well educated and generally considered the most fearless men in the employ of the Rio Grande - men who had caught runaway trains on the mountain side without so much as a flush suffusing their cheeks.

For nearly two months they were on the train, back and forth every other day and while the alternating crews had changed several times, they had not as yet seen the mysterious train, the sight of which had been the cause of so many engineers quitting that division.

One evening, just at dusk, while the fireman was lighting the lamp, the engineer, Edwards, experienced a strange feeling creeping over him and as he pulled into the canon, the silence seemed deeper than usual, the night darker and the air colder. Several times before they reached the grade the "popping" of the safety valve caused him to start. But soon they were winding in and about the labyrinth of small canons and over deep arroyos, and as his trained eye swept the glittering rails ahead, he forgot his uneasiness. Engineers seldom speak to their firemen - as a rule they are too busy; the constant watching requires that their minds should be on their work and tonight Edwards was more like a sphinx than usual, for it was reported that there was a bridge in danger of going down and a defective rail in one of the canons and ever and anon, he slackened the speed of his train as a matter of safety.

The engineer passed under a snowshed and the strange roar, so peculiar on such occasions, followed. While in the shed, far away there came the long, warning

whistles of an approaching train. Edwards remarked to his fireman that No. 8 was following too close. Again, when about five miles farther on, he recognized the same whistle, this time nearer, and at short intervals the signal was heard coming rapidly nearer.

"It must be a wild train." Whitehead grumbled, as the engineer reached for the rope and gave two short, sharp whistles only to hear the long dangerous answers. Again in a snowshed, it occurred to him that he had to "saw by" an east-bound freight at the next switch twenty-five miles farther up the mountain and as he left the shed, the bell sounded three times. He brought his train to a standstill as quickly as possible. He could hear the doleful sound of the followers as the piston rods traveled back and forth in the cylinders in the crisp night air, but a sound more ominous than that was the long drawn whistles of the engine that was so rapidly overhauling him. The conductor ran forward at this juncture and asked: "What did you stop for?"

"What did you pull the bell-cord for?" rejoined Edwards.

"You're crazy." the conductor said, "Now, pull her wide open and light out for the switches because we've got to pass No. 19 there and besides there's a wild train a-climbing up on us. D'ye hear?"

Edward drew back the lever with a strange feeling. He opened the throttle, the wheels slipped on the steel rails, but as they caught the sand, the long, heavy train began to move forward slowly. Both men in the cab could hear the sand grind beneath the enormous weight of the engine. The train increased momentum as it moved forward and in about five minutes was running as fast as practicable on that portion of the road.

The following train was approaching nearer and nearer. Again the short series of warning whistles was heard, which Edwards answered, but only to hear the wild train give the danger signal again. He looked out of the window as he was rounding a curve and noticed the other train rapidly approaching.

Cold beads of sweat stood out on his forehead as he pulled the throttle wide open. Faster and faster the speed of the train increased and more dangerous was the track. They were now in the very worst portion of the pass, where the snowbanks were the most treacherous and just in this part of the track was where the broken rail was reported. Every time the engine struck a curve it seemed as though it was impossible for the small flanges to hold the engine to the rails.

The cars were rocking violently. The train was lurching frightfully. The passengers were rudely awakened from their slumbers by the train striking a snowdrift. The speed of the train was so great that it broke the drift easily and was soon roaring through the snowshed. How the fireman labored; his shirt was wet with perspiration, for the hungry furnace consumed the coal so quickly that the stack belched fire.

FDS 92

The passengers, having been warned of the impending danger, had dressed themselves. The women were wringing their hands in despair, strong men were trembling and the thought of every person on the train was of the man whose hand rested on the throttle of the engine ahead. Would he be able to outrun the pursuing train and break all the snow banks, or would the rear train dash into the coaches and kill all the passengers? Who was their engineer? Was he competent? Was the engineer in the rear train mad? The curtains were all thrown up; a few daring men clung on the platform and glanced anxiously back.

The conductor started suddenly as he caught a glimpse of the driving wheels of the rear train. They were fully ten inches larger than those on the engine ahead. With hand tightly clinched on the throttle, Edwards' eye rapidly swept the track. He was a good engineer, for even under that awful strain, he had the presence of mind to shut off his steam in order to save it when running down grade without brake pressure and never once while running, did he allow power to take the place of speed, a fault of most engineers under excitement.

At this time the snow began to descend, and in the peculiar light that settles on the earth, caused by the snow, Edwards saw something in a backward glance that

made his blood freeze and almost caused his heart to cease beating. On the top of one of the cars of the rear train was the tall white figure of a man gesticulating wildly, while he could see a white form in the cab.

A terrible thought flashed through his mind - the train, the peculiar conditions - it was the phantom train!

Without further parley, regardless of the broken rail, he dropped the lever another notch, and then as quickly as possible, but cautiously, he opened the throttle valve. His trained ear caught every sound his engine made and under the intense excitement, he once thought he heard the pistons grinding and the axle pound. What a wild ride it was in the night. It would be impossible to pass a broken rail at the terrific speed they were traveling.

He was leading the race by about 200 yards now, and as his train approached a point where the track reversed and ran parallel, he nerved himself for the trial. He rounded the curve safely and was moving back on the serpentine curve with the rapidity of lightning. As he passed the other engine, he saw two extremely white figures in the cab. The specter engineer turned a face to him like dough and laughed.

The ghostly fireman reached for the cord and again a series of short sharp whistles sounded.

On the train plunged into the night, roaring through snow sheds and over iron bridges that trembled beneath the sudden shock. So fast was the train traveling, that the rush of air could be heard by the passengers. Wherever there was a snow drift, the train would break though it like a hurricane. Faster and faster, for now they were mounting to the highest point of the pass, where the air was coldest, steam was not so plentiful and soon Edward had the lever in the corner and the throttle wide open. The greatest speed his engine was capable of had been attained and Edwards could but watch the rails in front of him and keep his hand on the throttle.

The phantom train was gaining; he could go no faster; he was helpless. Around the shelves of high mountains and along the ridge of lofty hills, over deep arroyos, through long snow sheds, the race continued; the very landscape was closing behind the train like a cloud, the mountains seemed to recede rapidly, but all the while the specter train was gaining ground. The wind arose and sighed and from the north, heavy clouds began to drift southward. The pilot struck a slight snow bank and hurled it a hundred feet high.

A terrific storm was soon in progress, the furies of which seemed to concentrate on the fleeing passenger train. On into the night the train swept, specter and passenger, like bolts of lightning pursuing one another through the sky.

Edwards sighted a bridge that was reported weak, passed it safely and having by this time crossed the summit, was now on the down grade. Steeper it became and when one particularly heavy hill was reached, for the first time in his life, Edwards was guilty of running the grade without applying the air brakes.

Soon, he sighted the switch. No. 19 was not there and with a madness born of excitement, he went tearing by like the wind. Another series of short, sharp whistles and an instant later the engineer saw a red lantern swinging in the right of way. He was running down grade, the thought of No. 19 ahead, he instinctively applied the air. The wheels stopped revolving but the train was still running over the snowy rails.

Far ahead he observed light, shadowy, fantastic forms and as the train drew nearer, he saw that they were repairing the track. They were spirits, and the next minute flying toward the ghosts on the track, passed through the crowd of ten or twelve, reached the curve beyond and Edwards ventured a backward glance.

He saw the phantom train run to a broken rail. The engine ran off onto the ties and one second later, the heavy freight pitched down the embankment and a moment later vanished.

Written in the frost of the fireman's window was the following, in a peculiar hand:

Edwards passed No. 19 at the second switch, reached Green River at 6 o'clock the next morning, an hour ahead of time and left the Rio Grande that day. The following evening, he went to Salt Lake and went back to Denver over the Union Pacific on which he is now running and is considered one of the most trustworthy men in their employ. The phantom has not been seen since that eventful night.

Reprinted with the permission of the Rocky Mountain News who originally published this story on May 5, 1889

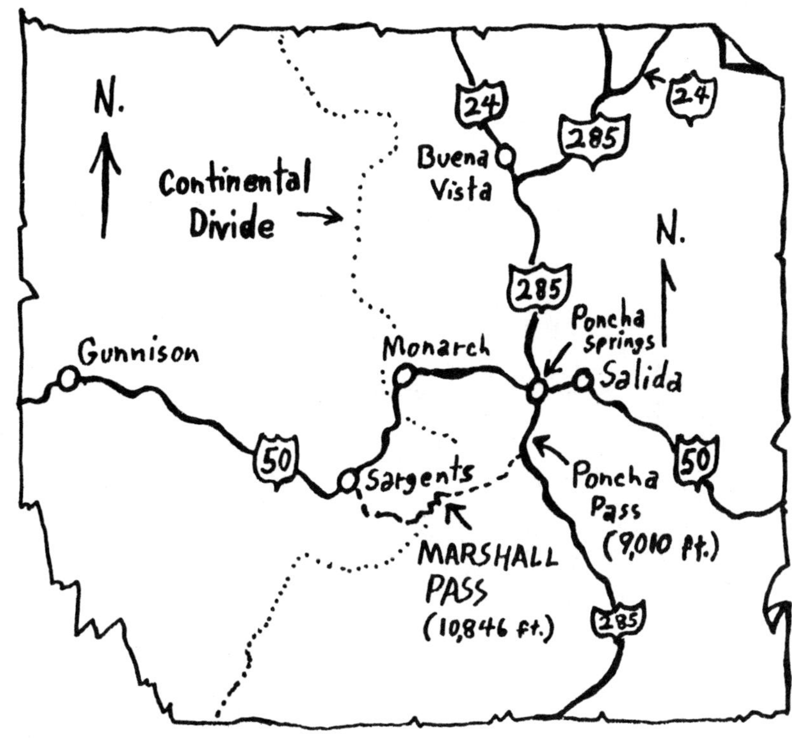

1. Marshall Pass: Located along the Continental Divide between Poncha Pass and Sergeants, Marshal Pass (10,846 Ft.), was first discovered in 1873 by Lieut. William Marshall, U.S. Army Corp. of Engineers. Marshall had been on a surveying trip to the San Juan Mountains and was returning home for the winter when he was struck by a severe toothache. In agony, he needed to find a quick route over the Divide in order to reach a dentist in Denver. Luckily, he found the pass which still bears his name and he was able to save himself 125 miles.

As soon as possible, the "Marshall Pass Toll Road Company" was formed. Five years later, a road was built over the pass.

In 1881, the Denver & Rio Grande R.R. bought the toll road for $40,000 and the pass was used as a narrow gauge route between Gunnison and Salida.

The line was used by both freight and passenger trains for over 74 years. It was finally abandoned in 1955.

WAS IT A GHOST?

A gentleman from Leadville tells the NEWS a queer story that was current in the neighborhood of the Morning Star Mine and that had created some consternation among the miners.

A few days ago, a man was killed in that mine by the caving in of a lot of earth and rock and none of the miners aware of the fact cared to work in the place where the man lost his life.

A day or two after the accident, a German happened that way in search of work and was sent into the drift where his predecessor was killed. He had hardly been lowered to the bottom of the shaft before he began violently shaking the rope of the windlass and in reply to inquiries from the men above, he said that there was a dead man in the drift. Supposing that some straggler had fallen down the shaft during the night, the man was told to put the body in the bucket. Having signaled that he had done so, the men at the windlass commenced turning the crank and as the bucket reached the surface, they discovered that it was empty.

When the German came up at noon, explanations were demanded but he claimed that the men were trifling with him in stating that the bucket came up empty and insisted positively that he had placed a dead man in it. His description of the corpse agreed in every particular with the appearance of the miner who was killed in the drift, although the German was ignorant of any fatal accident having happened in the mine. After being informed of it, he declined to work there any longer.

August 8, 1879
Central City Daily Register

A HOUSE OF HORRORS

**Terrible Experience
of Some Travelers in the San Juan in a Cabin.
An Old Tragedy Repeated
Before Their Eyes by Ghostly Actors.
A House in a Beautiful Wood
that is Studiously Avoided by All.**

In the southern portion of the state, in what is now known as Archuleta County, is one of the finest natural parks in the world. Magnificent pines, lifting their proud heads 200 or more feet in the air, extend for miles in every direction, with the imposing Needle mountains[1] for a background. The peculiarity of this park is that there is no underbrush beneath the trees and the green sward extending as far as the eye can reach makes vistas of sylvan loveliness through which the eye could rove for hours.

Far in the depths of ***this ideal forest*** was a cabin, by whom erected or for what purpose is a little uncertain, but possibly it was merely intended as a shelter for hunters of deer and elk, many of which are yet found in this magnificent forest.

In the early summer of 1880, a party of surveyors on their way to the San Juan, whose wonderful mineral resources were just becoming better known and about which many stories, reading like fairy tales, were told to excite the covetousness of adventurous spirits throughout the country, struck a trail through the timber and arrived at the lonely cabin shortly before nightfall.

The party consisted of the four surveyors and two miners named Tom and Jim Fulton on their way to the Needle mountain mines. As a beautiful little stream trickled over the rocks hard by, pouring its cool liquid fresh from the mountain snows, soon running like a silver thread over the emerald earth, then leaping over some tiny precipice in ***a beautiful***

cascade, the travelers resolved to camp there for the night and accordingly, a frugal supper was cooked and eaten, the blankets spread on the floor of the cabin and the arrangements for the night completed.

The surveyors retired early, but the Fultons sat up for a long time engaged in conversation. Tom was an old miner, who had prospected in the San Juan[2] some years before, but his brother Jim had only just arrived from their native state of Massachusetts having been written for by his brother, whose glowing accounts of the country induced Jim to leave his employments in the East and join his fortunes with those of his more experienced brother.

The night was a beautiful one. The moonlight filtering through the tall trees like tiny shafts of silver and both men, as they sat there smoking, were strongly impressed with ***nature's quiet grandeur.***

"I'll tell you, Jim," said the elder brother, "this is a beautiful country, but some terrible things have been done in it and many a poor man has lost his life. Why, it was only a little over a year ago, on my first trip to the Needles that somewhere in this very timber, a cruel murder was committed and the whole country was aroused and pursuit made of the murderer, who was followed clear to the mountains, caught, brought back and hung to a tall tree just in front of the cabin where the deed was done and which was something like this one. The murder was peculiarly atrocious, a man's mining partner having been slain by him in the cabin where they were both sleeping."

After some other reminiscences of mining camps and frontier life, the brothers retired.

It was perhaps midnight when ***a horrible, blood-curdling cry*** was heard ringing through the cabin and far out into the forest where it was echoed again and again on the night air.

Instantly the sleepers were awake, and sitting up, saw a terrible scene enacted

in the center of the cabin and only a few feet distant. Two men were struggling on the floor and presently the larger and more powerful getting his antagonist under him plunged a knife into his heart. The weird scene, lit up by some supernatural means, lasted but a few moments; the light died out and all was again still, save the heavy breathing of the frightened men, who were still looking with staring eyes at the spot where the tragedy had been enacted.

"It was Big Dan and his victim and the cabin is haunted." said Tom in a husky whisper. "Let's get out of this."

In a moment the horrified party were out on the green with their "traps". Not a sound was heard except the mournful cry of a whippoorwill and the soughing of the wind in the tall branches of the trees. While they were deliberating outside the cabin as to the next step to be taken, one of them exclaimed in a startled voice, ***"Look, what is that hanging there?"***

The now thoroughly frightened men looked up and on the tall branch of a tree distinctly saw, swinging to and fro in the faint moonlight, the body of a man hanging. This last sight at once determined their future course and it was only the work of a few moments to pack up blankets and baggage and start through the forest with only the one desire to put the greatest distance in the shortest space of time between themselves and the ghostly charnel house of terrors they had just left.

Their story was told in all of the camps which they afterward visited, and the haunted cabin still stands in the beautiful woodland glen, shunned, especially at nightfall, by all travelers on their way coming from and going to the hills.

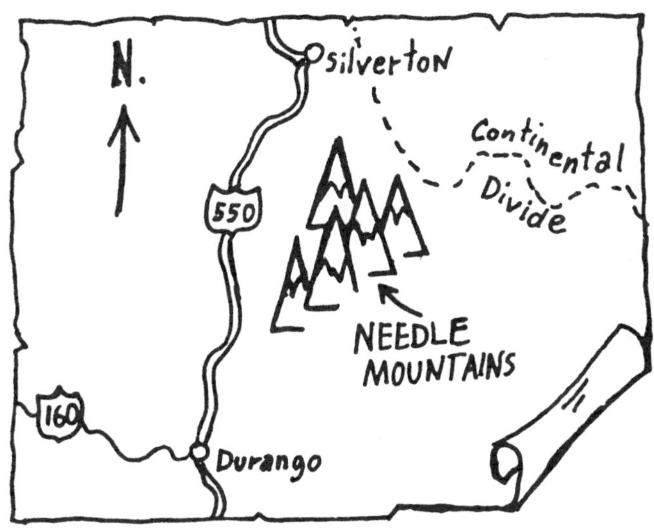

January 20, 1886

Reprinted with the permission of the Rocky Mountain News.

1. Needle Mountains: Located within the San Juan Range, they are described as having more "vertical topography" than any other mountains in the state. Because of their remoteness, the Needles are still a largely wild and unpopulated area.

2. San Juans: Covering most of southwestern Colorado, the San Juan mountains were once described as "the highest, most rugged and impracticable of all the Rocky Mountain ranges.

First explored by the Spanish before 1800, the San Juans contain some of the highest peaks in the state. Among the better known are Uncompahgre (14,309 ft.) Sneffels (14,150 ft.) and Chama (12,027 ft.)

MINER'S SUPERSTITIONS

Like sailors, miners are proverbially superstitious. Both miners and sailors, as classes, are usually ignorant of book lore, although neither are, by any means, as a rule, ignorant people. The latter are constantly journeying from one part of the globe to another and the information which they acquire from observation is very considerable; in the same way, miners are great travelers, living first in one place, then another.

From Cornwall, Wales and Bohemia, they come to Pennsylvania and Lake Superior; from Lake Superior and Pennsylvania, they journey westward to Montana, Colorado or Arizona and thence, perhaps, further westward. A new mining camp, with the excitement that it produces, draws miners from all parts of the country.

In 1878 and 1879, men came from the mines of Pennsylvania in the far east, from Lake Superior, from the lead mines in Missouri, from California in the far west, and from Nevada, to the (then new) bonanza camp, called Leadville.

In Colorado, prospectors are ***constantly roaming*** from one part of the state to another; miners are now working in Gilpin and Clear Creek, then in Leadville and Aspen and then, perhaps, in the San Juan.

People in the habit of making such extensive immigrations, are bound to accumulate vast stores of knowledge: although their erudition may be small, their education may be great. But although familiar with the phenomenon of nature, not being familiar with the laws by which they are governed and the causes by which they are produced, many seem incomprehensible. Some are considered supernatural and consequently are regarded in a superstitious manner.

The solitude of a sailor while cruising the boundless deep has much to do with his superstitions; men always feel safer in the company of their kind in the face of danger, either danger seen or the unseen feared. The miner while alone in the underground workings of a mine, is in as much solitude as the sailor in his ship.

The underground workings of an old mine, the old drifts and levels, the stopes, often immense chambers in the bowels of the earth, are always rather **weird and eerie places**. They have a musty, unpleasant smell from the decaying timbers. In

the gloom which the weak light of a candle produces, objects take grotesque and fantastic shapes. The old timbers, bulged and broken, are covered with white, mossy fungus. The roofs of old stopes sparkle with ice crystals when the candle light is directed to them. All is unearthly quiet, except when now and then one is startled by the cracking of timber directly overhead or on either hand.

The miners of Cornwall and Wales, Germany and Bohemia, peopled such places with gnomes and pixies and grotesque goblins; the miners of America, more enlightened, have no thought of such things, but in their superstition, believe that the mines are often haunted by the ghosts of the men who have been killed in them. It is no wonder that under the circumstances, strange unaccountable noises should be attributed to ghosts nor that queer effects of light and shade, produced by the faint, flickering light of a candle, should be laid to the same cause.

There is more than one mine in Leadville which is thus **said to be haunted**. There is one mine which, perhaps, bears the worst reputation of all. At one time, not long ago, it became so difficult to secure men to work in it that it seemed as if the company would be obliged to suspend operations. This, too, when the men working under him had a greater personal regard for the manager of the company than for any other mine manager in the camp.

There have been at various times several very unfortunate accidents in the shaft and the levels from it, whereby more than one miner has lost his life. So it has now come about, among the miners, that the mine is considered to be haunted.

There are said to be either two or three ghosts in the mine, which, according to the miners working there, especially haunt the first level, being met there more frequently than elsewhere. They do not make any particular rows or disturbances, these ghosts apparently not being of a malevolent disposition, but appearing more in sorrow than in anger. They are reported by the miners making curious noises in deserted portions of the mines and being altogether unpleasant apparitions to **meet in a lonely drift.**

One night two men were riding up the shaft on the bucket, when one of them turning, saw the ghost of a man who had been killed in the shaft only a short time previous, riding between them. The second man also perceived it and in their terror both nearly fell off the bucket, but regaining their senses clung to the rope. In the meanwhile, the bucket was slowly ascending the shaft, the ghost still standing on the rim and clinging to the rope, so that the two living men could feel his clammy hands. Just before the bucket reached the collar of the shaft, the ghostly apparition vanished. I do not know whether those men ever went down that shaft again or not, but I fancy not.

Four men were killed in a cave-in in the ___________ mine, several years ago and their ghosts still haunt the mine. They seem to roam about, now appearing underground and now on the surface, although they have not been seen at all now for some time. Once, one of them **was seen in the mill** looking for his brother, it was said, who was working there. The mill was running along smoothly, as usual, above the clatter of the machinery being heard the crunching noise of the rock breaker. Suddenly the latter stopped and down the steps came the rock breaker man with pale face; he had seen the ghost of his brother, who was displeased that he should still be working at the mine where he had been killed. This was certainly very unkind and unreasonable of the ghost, for the poor fellow threw up his job.

At one large mine of Leadville, which is worked through an incline, a man, Jack North by name, was employed to look after the rollers and rope in the incline. One day, while resetting a roller, the great skip came down unexpectedly and killed him. His successor was an old sailor, Bill Mar-line, who performed the duties of the position as usual for a while, but one day came rushing to the surface, panting for breath after his hasty climb, his face covered with beads of cold sweat. He said that he had been putting a new roller in the incline when he felt himself touched on the shoulder and turning, saw the **ghost of Jack North** pointing with outstretched arm up the incline. Marline, looking up too, saw the descending skip, almost upon him. He speedily jumped aside and made with all haste for the surface. He went down again

with the mine captain after telling his story, and the **roller was in its place**. Marline's story is firmly believed by the men of the mine. The officials, however, account for it by the theory that he was drunk which is not entirely improbable.

The underground men of a mine are not the only ones who have their superstitions. The managers and superintendents may not believe in ghosts, but there is more than one of them who believe that ore can be located by divining rods and electrical mineral indicators. There are some who believe in the one, some in the other; then there are, too, human "dowsers", whose hands swell in the vicinity of ore or show its vicinity by other manifestations. Some larger companies regularly employ these so-called dowsers and the amount of money that has been spent by their directions *is enormous*....here is a shaft sunk 800 feet deep; here is another 300 feet deep; here is a long tunnel or drift driven hundreds of feet through hard ground. They are all the work of "dowsers". It would be interesting to know exactly how much the credulity of mine managers has cost their companies in Leadville, for sometimes they do actually locate them.

If anyone is inclined to believe that such successes are evidences of some unknown occult power, in the soi-disant "dowser", let him prepare a statistical table and find the proportion of successes and failures. Even the occult power which the Yogis of India and Tibet claim to possess can not be used for their own pecuniary gain.

January 1, 1889
Leadville Herald Democrat

A CURIOUS CASE

**A Lawyer's Story of a Terrible Crime
and Its More Terrible Sequel
A Ghostly Visitant and Strange Deliverance
of an Innocent Man
An Injured Woman Confesses the Crime
and Kills Herself in Court**

"It was, perhaps, the strangest case that I ever had." said Judge Williams, musingly, as he watched the smoke curling from his cigar. Several lawyers from different portions of the country who had been drawn to Denver by a large mining suit before the United States court, in which there were many and diverse interests and an enormous amount of money involved, were sitting in the rotunda of the Windsor Hotel comparing notes and telling of strange experiences at the bar. Judge Williams was known to have had some of the most important cases ever tried in the state and was looked up to by the younger members as a man of ripe experience, whose advice on all legal subjects was valuable.

The rest drew their chairs close to where the judge was sitting and listened attentively as he proceeded:

"Yes, there were elements in the case and incidents, which I have never been thoroughly able to account for or explain to this day. Jack Wilson had been found ***murdered in his cabin*** , near the Eureka[1.] mine, under circumstances of the greatest atrocity. The head and arms were entirely severed from the body and numerous stabs from a huge hunters dirk had perforated the chest in a number of places. Suspicion was at once directed to a man named Christie Johnson, a Swede with whom he had had a lawsuit about some mining property and got worsted. Johnson was promptly arrested and placed in jail, making a narrow escape from being lynched by the infuriated miners, among whom Wilson had been a great favorite.

Johnson's friends at once sent for me and being at that time a new-comer in that section and being desirous of making a reputation, I took hold of the case with some alacrity and gave it every possible attention and study.

The case looked dark for Johnson. He had been seen in the vicinity of the cabin of Wilson late on the evening preceding the finding of the body. It was also known that he was the owner of a knife similar to the one probably ***used in committing the crime.***

He had entertained a bitter feeling against Wilson ever since the latter had gained the lawsuit against him.

I soon saw that the task before me was no easy one with this terrible array of circumstantial evidence and yet there was something in Johnson's appearance and manner that convinced me he was innocent, but, alas, how could I make this clear to the court and jury. Johnson explained his presence near the cabin on the fatal night by the fact that he had started for the mine to work on the night shift in the place of a man who was away, but after reaching the vicinity of Wilson's which was directly on the trail to the mine, he was taken slightly ill and concluded to return home. This statement, however, was not susceptible of proof, as no-one had seen him leave or return to his own cabin. As for the knife, that had mysteriously disappeared from his cabin on the day preceding the murder.

The affair worried me considerably. I could think of nothing else night or day. Even in my dreams numerous theories for the defense would form themselves, but be *as quickly dissipated.*

One evening, within two days of the trial and after I had just returned from a consultation with my client, being considerably exhausted by anxiety and throwing myself on a lounge in my office, I at once fell into a troubled slumber. How long I had been asleep, I know not, but I suddenly became aware of the fact that I was not alone. This knowledge was accompanied by a sensation for which I could not account. Opening my eyes I noticed that although the light in the lamp on the table had gone out, the room was illuminated with an unnatural glare, in the midst of which I distinctly saw the form of a veiled woman which approached me quite closely, but without raising the veil and said in a voice that was distinct although sounding as if from some far away place, "Christie Johnson is innocent of the crime of which he is charged." Forgetful of the strangeness of the affair, I excitedly asked the figure, "How can I prove it?"

"I will be at the trial and will give my testimony."

Although I was gazing intently at the presence, whatever it was, before I could open my mouth, *the figure disappeared* .

As soon as I recovered from my astonishment, I lighted the lamp and examined the doors and windows and found them securely fastened. This discovery increased the mystery in my mind to such an extent that I slept no more, but walked the floor the whole night.

The day of the trial at length arrived and found me almost totally unprepared with evidence of the innocence of my client. My sole hope was to make a strong appeal to the jury and to endeavor to impress them with my belief in his innocence. The court room was thronged by an eager crowd, attracted from the neighboring camps by the sensational and horrible details of the crime. The prisoner was brought in under a heavy guard and from the angry looks cast upon him, it was evident that in all that vast crowd, he had not a single friend.

Arraigned at the bar, the clerk said, "Christie Johnson, prisoner at the bar, you are charged with the **cruel and unprovoked murder** of Jack Wilson. What say you, guilty or not guilty?"

The hum of voices ceased and the room became perfectly quiet as the prisoner answered, "Not guilty."

Instantly, suppressed groans and hisses were heard from every portion of the house.

"Silence!" thundered the crier. The district attorney then proceeded to open the case in an address which laid special stress upon the horrible enormity of the crime and of the overwhelming testimony he would produce, proving beyond a doubt that the prisoner was one of the most hideous monsters that ever lived.

His speech was loudly applauded, after which the witnesses for the commonwealth were examined and gave damning testimony against the accused.

Finally, it came my turn to address the jury in opening for the defense. You can imagine what a hopeless task I felt it, with scarcely a single witness whose testimony amounted to anything. I made, however, what was probably the best speech of my life, pleading with all the power of words for the life of this innocent man at the bar, a victim of cruel circumstances and closed by warning the jurors that **the blood of a guiltless man** would be on their heads if they rendered a verdict of guilty on the purely circumstantial evidence of the prosecution. I then sat down.

Just as the judge asked me if I had closed for the defense, one of the tipstaves placed a piece of paper in my hand. I opened it eagerly and read, "Call Mary Powers." Turning to the court, I said, "May it please your honor, I have one witness to examine." and then handed the paper to the crier, who called the name loudly. At once I became aware of a slight commotion in the lower part of the room and saw the figure of a woman dressed in black and heavily veiled, which I instantly recognized at that of my midnight visitor, slowly making her way through the crowd. Arriving at the witness stand, she threw back her veil and exposed to view one of the most beautiful female faces, I had ever seen, whose classic outlines, however, were thin and careworn as with **the canker of an eternal sorrow.**

The interest of all in the room, which was centered upon the stranger, for no-one present had ever seen her before, was intense at this moment and was shared by judge, jury and attorney's; myself included.

Having been sworn, she told the following remarkable story:

"I was born in an eastern city and until a few weeks ago had never set foot in Colorado. When a girl of 18, I made the acquaintance of a young man of perhaps 24 years of age. He came to my father's house bearing letters of recommendation and we all liked him. Being of a handsome form and pleasing address, my fancy was captivated and his frequent visits to the house resulted in an engagement of marriage between us, but the wedding day on various pretexts was from time to time postponed. Meanwhile, presuming on my girlish innocence and want of a knowledge of the world, he caused my ruin and then basely deserted me, fleeing I know not whither.

For a long time I lay on a bed of sickness, ***hovering between life and death,*** in the frantic delirium of fever. Recovering at length, I became filled with one resolve - to search out my betrayer and destroy him. This idea haunted me so strongly, that the thoughts of a terrible revenge became the only joy left me. For several years, however, I could obtain no tidings of the betrayer. At last, however, my weary waiting was rewarded. By the merest accident, I heard of his presence here and came as an avenging nemesis. Upon my arrival by making cautious inquiries, I learned the whereabouts of his cabin and started toward it down the trail. I had not proceeded far before I noticed something shining lying on the ground. I stooped and picked up a knife - this knife." at the same time pulling from beneath the folds of her dress, Christie Johnson's knife.

"This incident perhaps hastened my revenge. With quickened steps, I soon reached Wilson's cabin and stealthily approaching the window, I saw that he was asleep. Cautiously pushing the door aside I advanced to his bedside and with a swift blow, ***plunged the knife in his heart.***

The sight of his blood maddened and infuriated me to a terrible pitch. Just what happened afterward, I could not tell, nor how I found my way to my quarters. In fact, I have but little recollection of what has since occurred, but I have had my revenge."

This was said with the laugh of a maniac and then quick as a flash, before she could be secured, she plunged the fatal knife in her bosom and fell to the floor with the life blood pouring from her breast.

A low cry of horror came from the spectators and all was intense confusion. Order at length being restored, the body was carried out and the jury, under instruction of the judge, rendered a

verdict of "not guilty" without leaving their seats. Johnson, considerably dazed by his unexpected deliverance and the tragedy which had just been enacted, was at once released and we left the court house together.

An inquest was held on the body of the dead woman and a verdict rendered according to the facts, but there was nothing upon her to show who she was, or where she came from. She was buried in a grove of pine trees near the trail and her story is often told to visitors at the camp."

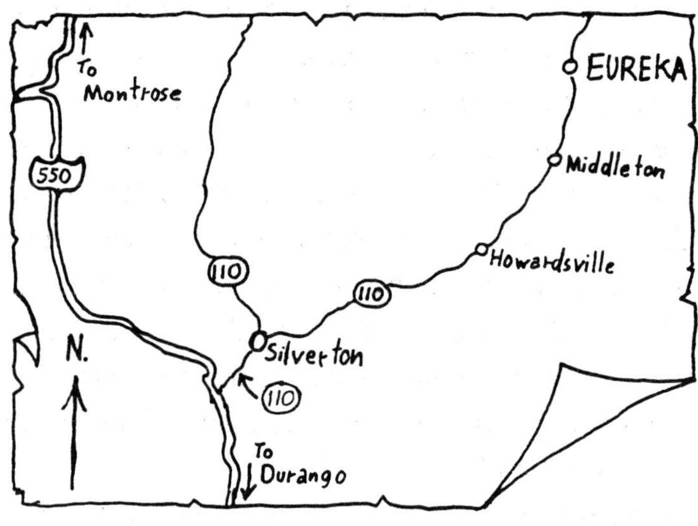

April 20, 1885

Reprinted with the permission of the Rocky Mountain News.

1. Like so many "boom towns" of that era, Eureka slowly withered and died after the mines played out. Today, with the exception of summer campers, it is "more or less" a ghost town.

SAVED BY A SPIRIT

The True Nature of the Lynching
of Jack Fillmore at Empire.
How The Ghost of a Murdered Man
Fastened Guilt on His Slayer.

Some question having been raised as to the justice of the noted Fillmore lynching at Empire[1.] in 1862, a NEWS reporter yesterday called upon Hon. George T. Clark, one of the principal actors in the tragic affair and was given by him what purports to be an accurate report of this prominent event in early Colorado history.

It will doubtless be flattering to the early pioneers to know that the statement of Mr. Clark fully refutes the assertion that the lynching was the result of an attempt to secure possession of a valuable mining claim as charged.

As to the nature of the supposed spiritual manifestation which Mr. Clark so firmly believes he experienced, of course a great deal may be allowed for the startling circumstances by which Mr. Clark found himself surrounded.

"It was not in '62", said Mr. Clark, "but in May '63 that the hanging occurred. The seventeenth of May. I am not exact about dates in general, but I shall consider my mental faculties on the decline when I forget THAT day.

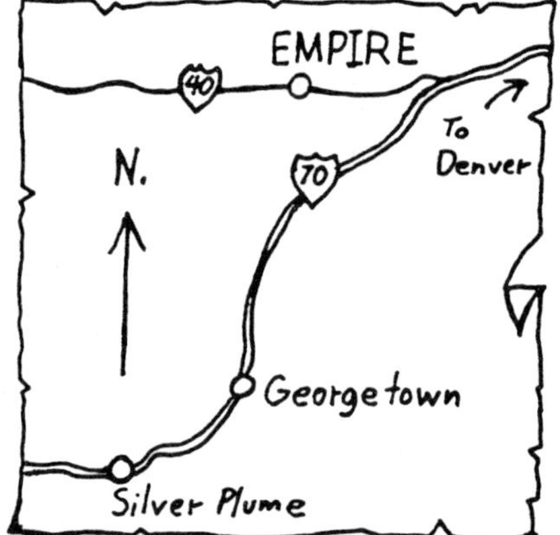

The excitement at Empire had been going on for some time and I had finally determined to try my hand at the new camp. I left Georgetown at noon on the sixteenth of May, going on foot and although the distance to be covered was but little over six miles, so bad was the road that it was quite midnight when I reached the new camp. I had got lost a couple of times on account of being unfamiliar with the road which was indeed but little better than a bridle path and when I reached Empire, I was fairly fagged out and about as anxious to get to bed as I ever was in my life.

I made a survey of the different hotels as the stopping places were called by courtesy, but with the only result of finding that I had arrived too late to stand any chance of finding a bed or even a place to stretch my bones. The shanties were absolutely crowded with the men who had been brought thither by the reports of wonderful gold finds in the new camp. The saloons and gambling places were running full blast, doing a land office business and I spent some little time in these in quest of a lodging place, but with no better success.

I had about made up my mind that not withstanding the inconvenience of the arrangement, I would have to camp out. It was not a pleasant prospect as the weather at that altitude, even in May, is decidedly the reverse of sultry. I was in one of the saloons pondering upon the unpleasant prospect before me and yet lingering in the grateful warmth of the fireplace, when I was approached by a tall man with

a heavy, black beard, who asked me if he had not heard me inquire for a place to spend the night. I said that he probably had, as I had made the request in at least a dozen different places since striking the damned camp.

"I know how you feel about it, partner," said he, "for I have been in the same boat myself at different times. But, it ain't a 'damned' camp any the more on that account. You see the camp wasn't got up with a view to providing you with a bed and if you've struck the place late, it's your fault and not the camp's and what's more, it isn't becoming to a young man to use such language."

I cheerfully apologized for the remark and was turning to leave the place in a last effort to find a lodging under some roof when I was restrained by my new acquaintance.

"What I wanted to say," he remarked, "was that if you wanted a lodging place real bad, I might find you a shake-down in my cabin until morning. There are three of us live there and if you'll be pleased to stop with us, you're welcome and if you don't like to, why there's no bones broken."

I assured him that I would accept his hospitality with only too great a pleasure. I was at first prejudiced against the appearance of the man, but his rebuke of my profanity, followed by this proof of his generosity, at once disarmed my dislike. He desired me to remain where I was until he would secure his partner. This took but a few minutes, the partner being engaged at a faro table in the room. On being called, the partner at once quit the game, but the two did not come to me at once, retiring to some little distance from the others, where they engaged in conversation of a very earnest nature. It struck me that the partner probably had some objection to my receiving the hospitality of the cabin, but I determined to let them settle the matter between them. The dispute was not of long duration, however, being ended by my new acquaintance taking a gold coin from his pocket, which the two proceeded to toss up. Three throws were made, the result being, as I judged, in favor of my new acquaintance. The other gave him a shrug of his shoulders and turned out the palms of his hands as an evidence of his acquiescence in the decree of fate. My acquaintance then beckoned me and I approached the pair. The new acquaintance was introduced to me as Jack Fillmore, his own name being given as Steve Langlade. The two led the way out of the saloon into the open air, when one of them, Langlade I think it was, drew from his pocket a flask of whiskey and requested me to take a drink. I did so and the bottle went around. Langlade requested me to sit down with him upon a log while Fillmore would go ahead and make arrangements with the third occupant of the cabin for me to occupy his couch with him.

Langlade and I sat down together and were soon deeply engrossed in discussing the prospects of the camp. He had a claim, of course, which promised to be one of the richest ever discovered and an interest in this could be had for a mere trifle comparatively. I was long enough in the country to take his statements at about what they were worth, but the bottle passed around quite lively and Langlade, I think, had the most plausible way with him of any man I ever met. I did not have that deep aversion to drink which I have since acquired as the result of my observation of its effects and I may say that after my tramp over the mountain I rather relished the bottle.

It was fully half an hour before Fillmore returned and when he did, he appeared to me to be laboring under strong excitement of some kind. He took Langlade aside a moment and the two conversed in a tone too low to be heard by me. They then returned to me and a short longer was spent in conversation and drinking.

Then we moved on toward their cabin. This was located at the end of a long row of similar shanties, standing some distance away from the others. Before we had gone half the distance, I began to find my knees grow weak and I was forced to lean upon Langlade for support. Before we had gone much further, both men were helping me along. An attempt at a song was the last recollection I have of the trip.

When I recovered my senses, it seemed as with a violent effort. I lay for some moments quite unable to move. Then I heard a low solemn voice by the side of the couch. I turned my face in the direction of the sound. A startling sight met my gaze. A tall young man with long yellow hair met my view. His face was that of a corpse and the front of his raiment was covered with blood.

I was not frightened in the least by the appearance of the figure, although I was fully impressed with the belief that it was not human. I was given no time to ponder upon this, for the spirit repeated, in solemn tones, "A murder has been committed in this cabin to-night and I am its victim. Less than an hour ago, John A. Fillmore drove your knife to my heart. You will find it in my body there."

I turned to the body which lay beside me and there saw the exact counterpart of the apparition before me, but still and calm in death. The ghost went on, "It is the design of Fillmore and Langlade to make it appear that you did the deed and it was for this purpose that they brought you here to-night. They are now engaged in jumping my claim, which they desired to get possession of. Later, they will return here and claim that they found you had killed me, and have you lynched. Take your knife and go. To-morrow tell at the inquest what I have told you. The time of the jumping of my claim by Langlade and Fillmore will be sufficient to convict them."

Then the apparition vanished. I did not wait a moment, but grabbing my knife, which Fillmore or Langlade had evidently stolen from my belt, I fled from the cabin. When the murder was discovered in the morning the camp was thrown into wild excitement. The murdered man was known to have made the richest strike in the camp and was, consequently, well known.

A rude inquest was held which was attended by every man in camp. I was in the crowd but managed to keep well out of sight. Langlade and Fillmore were the chief witnesses. They told a story which would have certainly hanged me if I had been found with the corpse. This was practically all the testimony bearing on the case excepting what I had to give and I had to give it. I felt that I owed a duty to the murdered man to see that his death was avenged and there was an irresistible impulse driving me on.

"I have something to say," I said, stepping forward. I then went on the stand and related exactly what had occurred.

"The matter is easily decided." said the foreman of the jury, "If the claim as been located by Langlade and Fillmore, it's a pretty clear case."

The jury adjourned to the location of the mine and there, sure enough, it was found that two men had relocated the claim. The inquest was adjourned shortly and Fillmore and Langlade were promptly strung up. The name of the murdered man as near as I remember was Casper Borgelt.

March 3, 1884
Reprinted with the permission
of the Rocky Mountain News.

1. Empire: A small mining town in Clear Creek County,
50 miles west of Denver and 4 miles north of Georgetown.

A SPOOK AT LAFAYETTE

Ghost Seven Feet High in the Traditional White
Boulder, Colo., March 9, -(Special)-

The citizens of Lafayette are much excited over the appearance of a ghost at the Burlington & Missouri station-house[1] near Lafayette. It is said to be white, about seven feet high, broad shouldered and heavy-chested. A few nights ago one of the men at the station-house saw it and fired at it, but merely succeeded in shattering all of the windows.

At another time, another boarder saw it and fired, but the ghost was unharmed though the door showed where the bullet had hit.

Last night, a dozen Lafayette people in answer to the summons "Come over and help us," went to see the ghost. It appeared at midnight. Those who saw it felt a cold, frigid feeling in their backs. The city marshal became paralyzed and his hat was lifted from his head. Tonight another big crowd will start for the haunted neighborhood to see if it can not be rid of the unwelcome spook.

LAFAYETTE'S GHOST
An Apparition That Makes a Nightly Appearance.
Lafayette, Colo., March 10. - (Special) -

Last night at 9 o'clock, this place was deserted, the people having gone to the Burlington & Missouri station-house to see the ghost, which makes its appearance there about 10 o'clock every night.

The ghost is described by one who was within ten feet of it as being that of a woman, whose neck and shoulders were bare. The features could be distinctly seen.

Several years ago, a lady was killed at this place, upon what was then the narrow-gauge railroad.

The ghost enters the house, so the story runs, and goes up the stairway. It was first seen by a little child.

Both stories originally published in The Denver Republican, March 10 and 11, 1893.

1. Sadly, the station is no longer standing. Even the railway line it served is soon to be abandoned. (1991)

A GUNNISON GHOST

The Sad Story Told by a Veracious Miner
to a Stage Driver, Who Knew the Ghost.
A Foul Murder and a Conscience Stricken Suicide.

There is a lonely spot in the Gunnison country not yet penetrated by railroads, but through which a stage passes at stated intervals. Stage drivers dislike to travel through the place at night, for they claim that the horses suddenly stop before a ravine in which stand the ruins of a burned cabin. Nothing in the shape of ghost or unnatural appearance has ever been seen to warn or frighten the beasts or the traveler, but a sense of something uncanny seems to lie around the spot as if .....

"Over all there hung a cloud of fear.
A sense of mystery the spirit daunted.
And said, as plain as whisper to the ear,
The place is haunted."

An old stage driver named Sam Eckefelt gives the following explanation of the feeling that effects the traveler. He says that for the few years that a stage line has traversed the spot the same phenomena have been observable at nightfall. The night may be still **as the heart of the dead,** but whenever the stage draws near the spot, a sudden whirlwind springs up and a dense fog seems to settle over nature. The horses always stop and it is with the greatest difficulty that they can be induced to start again. The sense of something near one, unseen but partly felt, comes to the mind. What this something is it seems impossible to determine. Sometimes it seems as if a cold hand passed over the face of the one who waits but a moment on the dreadful spot and the wind seems to carry a voice, low and muttering. Sam avers that he has several times smelled blood in the air, as his horses have stopped and that he has heard a sound of a steel knife striking against a piece of rock. Sam always declares he knows nothing about the history of the place, but Jabe Brown, an old miner who has traveled all through the mountains tells this story and has told it more than once to Sam Eckefelt without variation or change.

"About fifteen years ago, when the Gunnison began to be first settled, I had a friend in California Gulch named Joe Sommers. Joe got disappointed in the gulch and started off to locate some new claim he said he didn't care much where. He fell in with another fellow named Frank Elder. Elder was rather of a weak, sickly fellow, **a kind of a tenderfoot** , but was bent on making a fortune. I never could see how he and Sommers could jibe very well together. Sommers was a rough sort of fellow but with a big heart and was rather too fond of whiskey. Somehow or other the two drifted into the Gunnison country. They roamed about for a year or more and at last concluded to settle down in a place they christened Desolation Gulch. It was a wild, rough sort of place and mountain lions and Indians used to swoop down once in awhile and sneak off with their grub. But, they built a cabin and went to prospecting. Sommers somehow thought the place looked well.

They dug away at a prospect hole, but nothing seemed to pan out. At last, one day while Elder was lying sick in the cabin and cursing Desolation Gulch and his own bad luck, Sommers struck a lead. He told Elder of it and the brave young fellow jumped out of his bed, put on his pants and boots and started out to dig. In a short time, they saw their efforts rewarded and in a few weeks they had dug up a good quantity of ore.

In about two months they thought they had stuff enough on the dump to be worth quite a little pile and were going to start off to the nearest smelter. They had already loaded a train of burros with ore when in some way or another, they fell to talking on a division of the profits of the dump and Sommers said "Elder, I'll be damned if you are entitled to an equal pile with me. You were lying sick like an old woman in the cabin when I struck this lead."

Elder said quietly, "Joe, I don't want to quarrel with you, but I got off a sick bed to work on that lead and I think, old pard, you ought to let me have half the profits."

Then they got into a discussion in which I suppose pretty high words were used on both sides. Finally Sommers, having become thoroughly mad, said with **_a big vein swelling_** in his forehead, "You ____ ____!" I'll teach you what sort of divvy there is going to be in this outfit." and drawing a stiletto from his belt, he jabbed it quicker than lightning into Elder's heart. The poor little fellow sank back dead, never speaking after the fatal lunge was made.

The stiletto had been given to Sommers by a little German girl he used to be sweet on in Cincinnati. When she gave it to him, she told him never to use it except in defense of his own life or a woman's honor. He felt that he had not done either in this case and seizing the weapon, he smashed it against a stone, breaking it in halves. He then went  up to Frank to see if he was quite dead. It didn't take long to convince him that this was the case. His conscience was beginning to trouble him a little and he began to realize that he had acted pretty hastily in the little dispute. But outside of all that squeamishness about the murder, he was that mean to take up a business-like view of the matter and he thought to himself that he would now have the whole claim to himself. The next thing to think of was how ***to get rid of the dead body*** .

He thought on it a while and then concluded to stick it in a pool of water that lay about ten rods from the cabin. He thought he would leave it there till he got back from his trip and then bury it. He came down to Denver, got his money for the ore and started to enjoy himself.

One night when he was taking in the town with an outfit of tricked up acquaintances, of a pretty hard appearance, he comes into a saloon on Blake street and there he meets me. "Hello old pard." says I. "When did you get in?"

"Oh," says Joe, "I've been here a few days." Then he added, "I am pretty drunk to-night and I want to shake this ground. Help me on to do it, will you?"

"All right," says I. "Barkeeper, hear you got a little back room where my pard and I can talk things over a bit." As I did so, I jingled some coins in my pocket and added, "We have got the dust and we want to tackle some bug-juice and talk over old times."

"All right." says he. "Here, Tom, show these gentlemen a back room."

The other fellows who had followed Joe into the bar wanted to go out with us, but I looked round and says, "No, this is my ante and I want to keep you out."

The fellows were for kicking up a row, but the barkeeper says, "Gentlemen, I don't want no fighting inside. Go out on the street if you want to fight."

He started from behind the bar and an ugly looking fellow, who I suppose, was the bouncer, sprang out of a corner of the room. In the midst of the threatened scrimmage, Joe and I skips into the back parlor and ordered the drinks. Then we drew out our pipes and began to smoke. I could see that Joe was pretty drunk and very free to talk.

"Where's your pard Elder?" says I.

Joe kind of turned away his head and says, "Bill, I don't know where he is, so help me ____", then he stopped. He didn't seem to want to say God and I have thought since, he had better have said the devil. "You see," he added, "Elder wandered off and got lost. I haven't seen him for some time. He was bent on prospecting in a new spot."

I saw that Joe hung down his head while he said this and somehow though he was an old side pard, I didn't believe him. I said, "Joe, it's rather funny a man should wander off in that way and you not know where he is gone."

Then Joe said, "You know Elder was a queer duck anyway, a puny sort of a cuss, not much fitted to roughing it. He had a fever down there in the gulch and was sort of out of his head some of the time. He used to rave at times, about finding gold higher up in the mountains, and so one day when I had gone down to the nearest camp for some grub, he wandered away and I haven't seen him since nor heard from him."

I looked up kind of suddenly and caught Joe's eye. I says to him, "Joe, you and I have been friends for nigh on to six years, but I believe in my heart you're lyin'."

He says to me, "No, Jabe, honest to God, I ain't."

Between whiles, Joe and me had been drinking pretty freely and as I looked at his face, I began to fear he was going to have the jim-jams. "Yes," says he, "poor Frank, he and me never was cut out to get along well together. He was pretty flighty and you can bet your life I have got a quick temper and used to sometimes take him down when he got on his high horse. "MY GOD, THERE HE IS NOW!" he suddenly exclaimed. I looked around the room, but could see nothing. I was a little full myself and I says rather sharply "D__n it, Joe, you're drunk."

"No." say he, "There's Elder looking at me. He's got Gretchen's stiletto sticking in his heart."

"Then he suicided, did he, Joe?" I said looking up.

"No," says he, "he didn't...oh, keep him off, he'll throw that dagger at me!"

Then Joe fell out of his chair, rolled over and had a fit. I called in the barkeeper and we got the man over to my room. I called a doctor and we brought him to. He was sick for a number of days and during that time, as he gradually come to know a little, he told me the whole story of how he killed Elder. He said he felt easier after he had told it and didn't care whether they lynched him or not. I told him very few people knew Elder in this part of the country and I didn't think anybody would take the trouble to tie him up on a cottonwood. I told Joe he had done very mean by Elder, but as long as he lived I never would preach on him. After he was dead I could not answer for it. I thought he ought to give Elder's friends half his property after he (Joe) was dead, that is, if he could ever find any of 'em. Joe said he was dreadful sorry and would do anything I told him.

He felt worse about Gretchen's stiletto than anything else. I asked Joe what he meant to do and he said he meant to go back to the place and bury Elder, but he

wanted me to go back with him. In a few weeks, when Joe got stronger, we went back and dog-gone my skin if the first thing we saw when we got into the hut wasn't a bed made up in the middle of the floor and something in it that looked just like a man. I was sober as a judge and hadn't drank a drop for some days.

I went up to the bed and knocked my fist down onto the figure. The whole thing collapsed and the bed was as straight as ever. We looked under the bed and hunted all around and about the cabin, but couldn't find nothing nor nobody. Well, we got Elder's stiff out of the water and it looked and smelt horribly. We buried it under a pile of stones and Joe says, "Now, d__n him, he can't come to life again."

That night, Joe and I slept together but somehow it seemed, all night, as if there were three of us instead of two, and in the morning when we got up and washed, we looked at our bed and it looked just as if there was a man there again.

Well, to make a long story short, Joe sold his claim to a Yankee in California Gulch for big money. The Yankee never saw any ghosts or didn't care for them if he did. He took out a lot of ore, made quite a nice pile, came down to Denver and got killed in a saloon fight. Joe went back east and found that his German girl had died of heart disease on the very night he had killed Elder with her dagger. Then he had a kind of sneaking curiosity to go back to the old hut and alone. I started to go with him but got drunk and was delayed a few days. When I arrived at the gulch, Joe was lying with his throat cut in the remains of the hut which I suppose he set on fire. His body didn't seem to have burned much though. I buried him near Elder but nobody has worked the claim since and never will. There is lots of big money to be made there yet, but somehow the place has got a bad name and nobody would dare to work it."

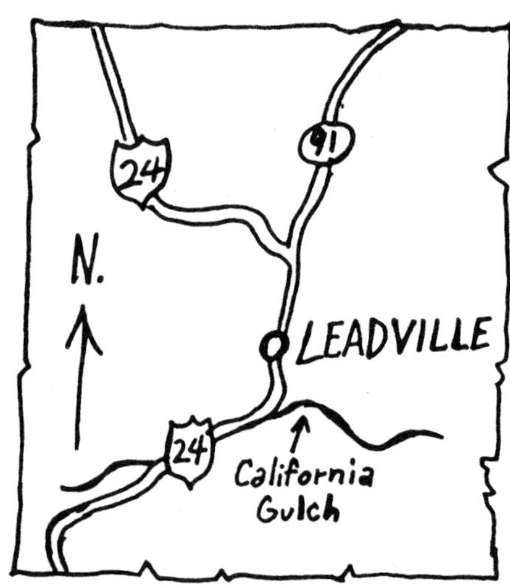

February 27, 1883

Reprinted with the permission of the Rocky Mountain News.

A MARVELOUS MYSTERY

**A Story of the Beautiful St. Vrain Valley
and Its Secrets, Which have Never Been Solved.
Mysterious Caverns
with Enormous Deposits of Mineral Wealth and Wonderful Features.
By Some Apparent Enchantment,
the Whole Scene Vanishes Like a Strange and Beautiful Dream.
A Legend of Aztec Customs
and a Possible Explanation of the Strange Sounds.**

In the heart of the Great Rocky Mountain region are scattered many beautiful parks which form much of the romantic scenery for which Colorado is famous. Probably the most remarkable of these great natural basins are located between the beautiful valley of the St. Vrain and the larger section known as Estes Park, which is becoming so well known to tourists and pleasure-seekers, although much of the territory is yet almost entirely unexplored, occasional glimpses only having been obtained by parties ascending Long's Peak[1.], from the side of which mountain monarch *the view is inexpressibly grand.*

A few years ago, Colonel Joseph T. Boyd, the governor's secretary, with a companion, was engaged in looking for a route with feasible passes and grades for the construction of the Denver, Utah and Pacific railroad, whose present terminus is the new and beautiful little town of Lyons situated forty-four miles from Denver in a little park of its own.

One morning, the two men broke camp early and started to ascend Long's Peak, both mounted on good and reliable ponies, whose intelligence in picking out the safest trails and best routes was considerably above the average.

They had not proceeded very far before they descried as they turned the corner of some rocks in a southeasterly direction what appeared to be *a magnificent park* of whose existence they had previously been in ignorance.

"There was something so striking and peculiar in its location and general form," said Colonel Boyd, "that getting the bearings as well as we could, we retraced our steps and made our way along the banks of a stream as well as we could for the thick growth of cottonwoods which were in profusion on either side. It was several hours before we reached the borders of this park, when we discovered that it was surrounded on nearly every side by a high rocky wall, *which seemed utterly impassable.* We had to make a detour of nearly three-fourths of the entire circumference before we found an opening by which we could get in. This in itself was most peculiar and consisted of a tunnel or cave of considerable size and of some length, perfectly straight, and through which we could see daylight at the other end. The distance through it, I should judge, was about one-fourth of a mile.

Preparing to enter with our horses - the tunnel being high and wide - a new difficulty presented itself. The intelligent animals **would not enter the cave** despite our every effort at coaxing or driving. After numerous futile attempts, we dismounted and failing even to lead them, fastened them securely to some scrub oaks on the outside. The strange behavior of the horses and their trembling and excitement, I must confess, impressed us with an uneasy feeling at the onset, which was largely increased as we proceeded by some wonderfully strange noises we heard, as if proceeding from the park itself and which was reproduced with awful distinctness by the echoes in the cavern. These horrible sounds seemed a combination of cries, groans and shrieks, **mingled with hideous laughter.**

Trembling, we emerged at the other end and were inside of what we now felt was an enchanted place. The sounds which had frightened us so much seemed to die away in the distance and feeling emboldened, we strode across one of the most beautiful valleys I had ever witnessed. Along the banks of a murmuring brook whose waters were as clear as crystal, there grew in profusion some of the most gorgeous flowers ever seen. Following the tiny stream for about a mile, we came to its source, which was a fairy lake, fairly embowered in roses and flowers of every hue. At one end was a tiny forest like a bower of green, **a fit setting for the gorgeous picture.**

We advanced to the middle of this little wood and found a semi-circular bank, some ten feet in height, in the side of which facing the lake was an opening. This cave, for such it appeared to be, was something less than five feet in height, descending rapidly from the surface on a comparatively steep grade. We entered the mouth of it and were instantly saluted with a repetition of the same horrible sounds we had heard at our first entrance to the park, only seeming to be magnified one hundred times. In fact, the **supernatural dis-cord** was so awful that we were compelled to twice retreat before getting far from the mouth. The third time we pushed forward, ashamed to be driven back by mere sounds, and had gone perhaps a hundred yards when we became aware of a strange bright light. In what seemed a circular hall, lighted in some unseen way, was a mound composed of precious stones and rich bits of ore in which

gleamed rich seams of native gold and silver. As we advanced to the mound the din became perfectly unbearable. Voices, seemingly human, but in an unknown tongue, alternately seemed to coax, beg, implore and threaten by turns, the jabbering imploring tones would change to fierce threatening ones, seemingly pouring into our very ears *a huge torrent of incentive* endless as the waters of a rapidly flowing river. After a few moments we were compelled to retreat without being able to carry away a trophy.

Upon reaching the outer portion of the wood, we discovered that the sun was low down on the horizon and already the walls surrounding the park were casting their shadows over a large portion of the ground and we hastened on through the tunnel with the echoes of a million shrieks and groans pursuing us clear to the entrance. We found our horses where we had tied them, but *trembling as with a mortal fear.*

Hastily mounting, we hurried from the seemingly accursed place, fear adding speed to the horses feet. In a short time, we were several miles away and reached our camping ground just at dark. Throughout that whole night I could imagine the repetition of the horrid noises of the park, every whisper of wind through the trees being, to my excited imagination, a continuation of the horrid din.

When morning dawned and the sun arose over the hills at the east, I again felt brave and we agreed to go back again as soon as we had breakfasted and try to obtain *some of the wealth in the cavern.* Before starting, however, we looked toward the place of our adventure of the day before, but it seemed all a blank. A blue haze seemed to envelope every object in that direction and the whole landscape looked unfamiliar. We galloped off, however, taking the same trail as before, but very soon found that the country we were in, was a strange one, all of the signs and the landscape being unfamiliar. After traveling in what I am sure was the right direction for a number of hours, no trace of our enchanted park could be discovered

and I have since, frequently alone and in the company of others, sought for it, but in vain. *It would seem to have been swallowed up* and its existence remains with my companion and I as a strange, unexplainable dream.

I have endeavored in a number of ways to account for the adventure, but have yet hit upon no satisfactory solution of the mystery. An old Indian chief, whom I knew, told me of a legend of his tribe that, many hundred moons ago, there was a settlement in the park of a race of people resembling the white man of today. That they built houses, raised corn and knew many things of which the Indians were ignorant. One of their great occasions was a funeral, the ceremonies of which lasted for several days. ***The burial places were in caves*** and were tended and guarded with great care. A peculiar part of this custom was for everyone of the tribe and of visitors to contribute some valuable mineral or precious stone and lay it upon the grave of the dead to propitiate the evil spirits and ensure peace to the soul of the deceased. These deposits or mounds were regarded as sacred and it was believed that swift and certain death at the hands of the spirits would be the fate of any one who dared to remove them.

It could hardly be possible, however, that ***we had stumbled upon one*** of these ancient Aztec burial places, but what and where it was, has bothered me ever since. If I could find the place again, I might get a partial solution of the noises from the fact that in the park there is a strange bird sometimes seen in large numbers, evidently of the parrot species, as it is an incessant talker, making at times a horrible clatter.

I shall make another effort to find my enchanted park before the fall is over." said Colonel Boyd.

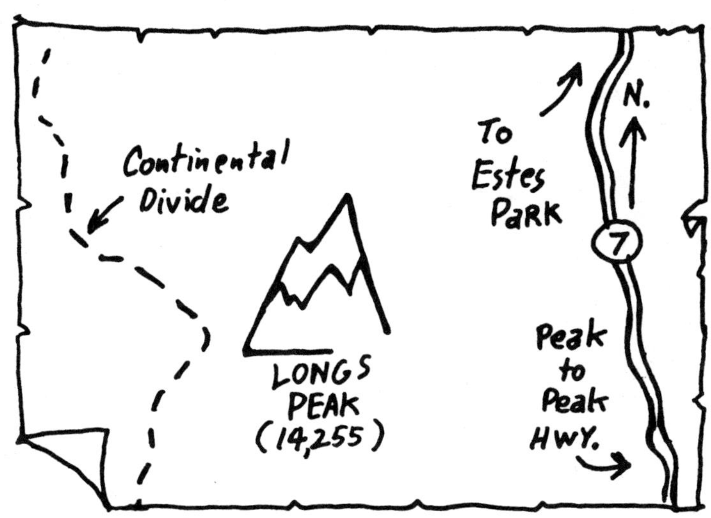

Sept. 29, 1885

Reprinted with the permission of the Rocky Mountain News.

1. Long's Peak: 15th highest peak in Colorado (14,255 ft.). Named for U.S. Army Major, Stephen H. Long.

HAUNTED GULCH

**A Rich Traveler Murdered in a Lonely Cabin
for His Money by Two Desperate Characters.
Superstitious Travelers Assert That the Murdered Man's Cry
of Mortal Agony is Still Heard After Nightfall.**

Coyote gulch, one of the numerous arroyos on the divide which during heavy rains become the course of raging rivers, in a few hours to become as dry as the surface of the surrounding hills, is situated right in the heart of the district which is now the scene of the gold excitement of Douglas County.

At the distance of a few rods from its banks stands a dilapidated cabin, a one-roomed structure originally built exclusively of logs but to which several apartments had been added of frame roughly constructed. At the present time, the place is in a state of decay, peopled only by the numerous families of swallows who live in absolute and un-disturbed possession. Nothing could be more lone-ly and desolate looking than this pitiful remnant of what was once a home. Stripped of its sheathing, the log wall of the abode stands out *like the ribs of a skeleton* from which has fallen its comely outer covering, between whose openings the storms pitilessly beat and through which the winter winds howl their requiems.

Thirteen years ago, the cabin and ranch upon which it stands were occupied by the McIntyres; father and two grown sons, together with the wife of the elder McIntyre and two children by a former husband. The reputation of the family in the sparsely settled neighborhood was anything but good and dark stories were told of unwary travelers who had sought shelter there for a night, but who had never afterward been seen.

One stormy evening in June, 1873, a stranger, supposed to be from Denver, who had missed the stage and had attempted to walk to Russelville, but who was overtaken by the storm, knocked at the McIntyre abode and asked for shelter for the night.

The house at that time consisted of the main log structure, two frame additions in the rear and a rude sort of loft over the principal room reached by a narrow flight of steps. The one window lighting this loft overlooked the roof of the low addition immediately in the rear, in which Jack and Jim McIntyre the two "boys" slept.

The knowledge of the ***terrible tragedy which followed*** was derived chiefly from the confession afterward made by Jim McIntyre. When the stranger, after the door was opened, had proffered his request, he was told to be seated, then the old man and his two sons went into a back room and had a long whispered conversation, at the end of which the father returned and taking a candle asked the visitor to follow him up the narrow stairs to the apartment above and showing him a rude bed, bade him good-night.

Soon his deep breathing which could be heard through the chinks of the floor in the room beneath attested that he was asleep. No sooner was this made certain than the two boys slipped outside, placed a small ladder against the lower building, gained access to its roof and thence to the room in which the stranger was sleeping, through the window which had been purposely left open. Stealthily advancing upon the unconscious sleeper, a blow with a knife was delivered with a swift and sure aim. Death, however was not instantaneous and there rang out upon the night air, up and down the gulch and far over the divide, such ***a cry of mortal agony*** as haunted its listeners to their dying day. Another deadly stab and all was over.

Upon examining the person and effects of their victim, the murderers found, as they had suspected, a considerable sum in money and gold dust, a costly gold watch and other valuables. Appropriating these, they lifted the body, while yet warm, with the blood oozing from the gaping wounds, through the open window, carried it down the ladder and thence to a thicket of oak brush a few rods to the rear of the house, when, hastily digging a shallow grave, they thrust the ghastly evidence of their crime into it, filled in the earth and covered the whole with dead leaves.

Several days elapsed and the murderers, after dividing the spoils of the dead man, were living in fancied security, until suddenly, one morning shortly after daylight and before they had arisen, the cabin was surrounded by a large body of determined men, armed and evidently bent upon an errand of vengeance. Entering the abode, the father and sons were quickly made prisoners, their arms pinioned and a strong guard placed upon them. A thorough search of the premises began and in the fatal loft was found ***damning evidence of the crime*** in the stains of blood in the bed, on the floor and casing of the window. Tracing the course of the murderers when removing the body by the clotted spots which had not been removed, the object of search was eventually found and disinterred and their horrible suspicions confirmed.

It seems that the stranger, who proved to be a prominent banker of Denver, had left for Pueblo with a considerable sum of money which he intended to use in the latter city, but leaving the stage at the first station for a few moments was for some unaccountable reason left by it and in his anxiety to reach his destination he started to walk to the next station of Russelville, thinking to obtain there some sort of conveyance with which to proceed on his journey. Upon the return of the stage to Denver, two or three days afterward, his mysterious disappearance was learned by his friends.

A party was organized and mounted on good horses, started on the road making inquiries everywhere. Learning at the station, where he had been left, the fact of his having started to walk to Russelville, they at once proceeded to that place and discovered that he had not been there.

Feeling convinced of foul play, and being aware of the bad reputation of the McIntyers, they resolved to make them a visit whose discoveries justified their worst fears. After disinterring the body, they returned to the house and found that through the negligence of the guards, Jack McIntyre, the elder brother, had slipped off his shackles and escaped. He was never captured, but from accounts published some years afterward, a man answering his description was lynched in a New Mexican town for killing another over a game of cards.

Ropes were placed around the necks of the old man and the other son and they were led down to the gulch, where a gigantic pine reached its long arms nearly across its bed. Jim McIntyre was given a sufficient time to make a confession, in which, after reciting in a cold-blooded manner the details of the horrible deed, from any participation in which, however, he exculpated his father.

He was swung off from one of the branches of the tree by strong and willing arms, thus meeting a swift punishment for his ghastly crime. The body was left swinging over the stream for some time and was then cut down and buried at the foot of the tree. Partly from Jim's strenuous assertions of his father's innocence and partly because of the pleadings of the latter's wife, he was suffered to go, with the understanding that he should at once leave the state, which he lost no time in doing with his family and has never since returned.

Travelers and cowboys, who have occasion to pass the deserted cabin after nightfall, stoutly assert that the agonized death cry of the murdered man can be heard every night, echoing over the hills and through this gulch, which, strange to say, is the heart of the gold district and has proven to be one of the richest placer diggings.

June 9, 1884

Reprinted with the permission of the Rocky Mountain News.

A QUEER STORY

A Notorious Woman
Gives Reason for Changing Her Mode of Life.
Warned by
a Supernatural Visitant in Pueblo - She Returns to Denver.
She is Now a Member
of the Salvation Army in Good Standing.

Two of the Salvation Army women were canvassing the city securing purchasers for the War Cry, the army organ. One of them, a very pretty girl, stepped into a Fifteenth St. store and asked the proprietor if he would not be kind enough to buy a paper of her. "It is only one nickel, sir." she said.

"Certainly," was the reply. "I will buy a paper of you and would if it were a dollar." He gave her one dollar and was warmly thanked for it. As she left the building with her companion and walked up Fifteenth street, the proprietor beckoned to a NEWS reporter across the street.

"I will tell you a good story about that woman, which is vouched for by those that know it to be true in every particular and if it is, the Salvation Army has certainly done some good in Denver.

The woman went by the name of Belle Grant about five years ago and was one of the hardest characters in the city. She had as a running mate a girl named "Lil" something, who was also a terror. They frequented saloons and were full every night."

FALLEN LOW

"Belle was the mistress of a notorious sporting character when she first came to Denver, but being capricious, changed her lovers with the regularity her kind are famous for. When drunk, she was quarrelsome, always carried a pistol and a knife and was not slow in cutting or shooting. She severely slashed several parties that I know of and sent one of her lovers from Denver with a bullet in his arm.

About six months ago, she telegraphed her friend Lil, who was living in Aspen, to come to Denver and they would go to Salt Lake City. Lil came in response to the telegram and the two started for the city of Latter Day Saints. Belle got no farther than Pueblo, but Lil went on to Salt Lake. Belle came back to Denver. The reason she returned, she says, was because she was warned by God in a dream that she was leading a sinful life. She says that, while in Pueblo, she had a presentiment that something was going to happen if she didn't get off the train and did so; her companion humoring her whim and consenting to remain in Pueblo that night."

128

A SUPERNATURAL VISITANT

"Belle asserts that when she went to bed, she had that uncomfortable feeling which one feels when satisfied that something or somebody is near him without being able to unravel the mystery. She lay awake until after midnight and was conscious that some impalpable thing, which at times assumed a human shape, was near her, and that several times it tried to speak to her. She dosed off into sleep, but was suddenly aroused by someone saying, "Belle! Belle!"

She sat up in bed, peered around the room, but could see nothing. She sat there frightened and trembling for some time, finally mustering up courage to lie down again and try to sleep. She closed her eyes and almost immediately the room seemed filled with light. She kept her eyes closed, but could see everything in the room plainly. A woman appeared whom she recognized as her mother, who had been dead for a number of years. She sat down on the side of the bed and placing her hand on Belle's forehead, told her she felt grieved at her wayward course and that she could never meet her if she did not stop her sinful career, which Belle promised to do. Next morning, Belle bade farewell to Lil, returned to Denver, where she has been ever since."

THOROUGHLY REFORMED.

"She rented a small room when she returned and I am told that for a long time afterward she was in the habit of lingering around churches when there were any services, not daring to enter, thinking probably she wouldn't be welcome. She took in plain sewing and conducted herself with as much propriety as the most strait-laced matron in the city. When the Salvation Army made it appearance in Denver, she attended the meetings for some time before she joined the army. She is now a faithful worker in the ranks."

"Do you think her conversion is genuine?"

"I am satisfied it is. She shall always have my assistance."

July 3, 1887

Reprinted with the permission of the Rocky Mountain News.

A HAUNTED SPRING

Strange Experience
of an Early Colorado Prospector in a Gulch Near Breckenridge.
A Curse Laid Upon a Pleasant Spring
by a Maiden Who was Stolen From Her People.
An Indian Legend
and What the Prospector Suffered for Disregarding It.
A Night's Vivid Horror
Graphically Related by the Sole Witness of its Occurrence.

"Did I ever tell you about the haunted spring near Breckenridge?" was asked by George T. Clark of a NEWS reporter yesterday. "No? Then I may assume that you have not heard of it as I do not know of any other white man than myself who has examined the spring with sufficient care as to be able to report upon it understandingly.

The Indian name of the spring is Pau-to-creeda, the literal translation of which is the Spring of the Maidens Curse. In one sense it is near Breckenridge, but in another, it is far enough away as it requires a day's journey to reach the spot. When I first visited the spring, it was in the fall of '59 and there was no Breckenridge there to measure from. I had started into that section of country at this early date under the guidance of an intelligent half-breed Mexican, who had discovered the presence of gold and silver there.

This guide was a strange mixture of characters, the super-stition of the Indian and the love of gold of the Spaniard being about equally blended. He was probably the son of some ven-turesome Spaniard or Mexican who had ventured as far north as the country of the Utes, from whom he selected a wife. He was raised among the Utes, but afterward received a limited educa-tion in Mexico. I never was fully convinced that his mind was wholly sound, but gave little thought to the matter.

I found him to be thoroughly sound in his knowledge of surface indications and cared little for the rest. He was a great talker and beguiled many a weary mile of our march with his relation of Indian legends, in all of which he appeared to have implicit faith.

131

We had been engaged in the work of prospecting near where Breckenridge now stands for over 2 weeks and had not yet discovered the great find which my guide, whose name was Martinez Armijo, had promised. On the morning of the eighth day, Martinez informed me that a lucky day had arrived and that he would venture to discover the sought for treasure. I had previously been quite unaware that he had been restrained by any superstitions, having been put off with one excuse or another from day to day. I had charitably supposed that he sought to lengthen out his term of service for the sake of his per diem, as many law-makers do. I was, therefore, much provoked at the idea of having been kept tramping around through the mountains for a week to accomplish what might be done in a single day and I gave Martinez a piece of my mind.

"Oh! But," he said, "you know nothing about the spirits who rule over the place where we are going, while I know them all. We must go by the Pau-to-creeda and the spirit of the spring is one of the most vindictive in all the land."

I satisfied myself by using some good old English oaths, which I knew he did not understand and which, I presume, he put down as an exorcism of the spirits.

We made a hard march that day, which was enlivened by no stories from Martinez. Whether it was his desire to get through with the work in hand on so favorable a day, or that he was reserving his powers for a struggle with the spirit of the Pau-to-creeda spring, I could not guess, but I certainly missed his harmless chatter.

The route taken was entirely different from any that we had hitherto traversed and was lamentably lacking in water. By noon I was thoroughly dry, my supply of liquid refreshments having received a serious draft in trying to revive the spirits of my guide and my own thirst had done away with the rest. Martinez did not appear to be greatly troubled by a lack of water, his thirst appearing to die out with the emptying of my bottle. We crossed several mountains, keeping the high ground as much as possible, notwithstanding my oft-repeated desire to strike down in search of a creek or spring. Martinez steadily vetoed all such propositions, claiming as an excuse that he could not reach the place sought excepting by keeping certain elevations in sight.

Toward sunset we arrived on a mountain overlooking a gulch which Martinez pointed out as the promised diggings. The gulch has long since given up its wealth of gold which was not inconsiderable but I confess that when I gazed upon it first, it was not with a view to finding whether the rocks were golden or not, but with a view to finding if it contained any water for by that time, my throat and mouth were fairly parched with thirst. The gulch is probably even yet as wild and picturesque a one as could be found in Colorado, notwithstanding the unsightly evidences of placer mining left by the long gone miners. Frowning precipices, gnarled pine trees and towering buttresses of granite were the general features, but I paid little attention to them, my eye having been caught by the glinting of sunbeams upon a

fountain of water which sprang from the opposite side of the gulch beneath an overhanging
rock. It may have been because I was thirsty,
but I certainly thought that I had never seen any
spot in the world half so lovely as that surrounding the spring. The rest of the gulch was
as devoid of vegetation as could be imagined
with the exception of a scraggy growth of pinon
trees where sufficient earth had accumulated
between the rocks to make a foothold for these
hardy pioneers, but around and below this
spring for quite a distance, the hand of nature

had done its most skillful work in the way of decoration. Vines clambered over the rocks while immediately below was a mound covered with grass which sloped away in such regular shape that it looked as though formed by the hand of man instead of nature.

I told Martinez to show the way down into the gulch, but he appeared extremely unwilling to do so.

"Why man," said I, "don't you see that there is water there?"

"I feared this." said Martinez. "That water which you see is cursed water. It is the spring of Pau-to-creeda. Those who drink of it once - and who has not? - never do so again."

"Curse or no curse," said I, "show me the way to the spring. Your fictions are pleasant enough when the bottle is full, but now that I am dying of thirst, I fear that I will have to defy your spirit of the spring."

Martinez threw his hands by his sides in a despairing gesture, relapsed into complete silence and then moved down into the gulch by a circuitous way, which by the way, has since proven to be the only way of reaching the bottom of that gulch.

When we reached the spring, the sun had already disappeared, but a delicious twilight reigned around. Amid the vines clustering over the rocks some little birds were twittering.

"The birds do not appear to fear your spirit of the spring," said I, "and I can see no reason why I should."

I stooped to the tiny stream of water which flowed from the large basin of rock in which the spring was located, but Martinez grasped me by the shoulder. He gazed into my face a moment and said, "You will regret it if you drink of the water of this spring. There is another farther down the gulch where you can drink in safety. Come with me."

But I laughed at his fears and tasting the water, I found it to be delightfully pure and sweet. I drank copiously from the spring and then turning to Martinez, I asked him to tell me the story of the spring.

"Not here," said Martinez. "I have been here longer than I care for. It will soon be night and we cannot get away too fast."

But I pooh-poohed the idea of leaving the spring, saying that I had not found as lovely a spot to sleep in since we had entered the mountains.

Martinez proceeded to prepare supper in a manner quite different from his usual lively way. He said but little, casting an eye every now and then at the spring as though he feared some hobgoblin might emerge from its rock-rimmed fissures. I noticed that he refrained from using the fuel from the trees and vines around the spring, but went to a considerable distance to secure drift wood. When our frugal meal had been dispatched, I again entreated Martinez to tell me the story of the spring. He did so, but not without some reluctance and in a hurried manner, quite unlike his usual style of narration, which abounded with detail. He said:

"I only know the story as all the Utes know it and have known it for generations, how many I could not guess. I know that no Ute ever drinks of the waters of this spring or meddles with it in any way without meeting with ill luck. There seems to be some fascination about the place, for it is visited by every man, woman and child in the tribe at least once in a lifetime and seldom oftener. I came here when a boy and drank of the waters. Three days later, I slipped on a trail a short distance from here and fell over a precipice, only escaping death by striking in the limbs of a pine tree. As it was, I had several of my bones broken and for a long time I hung between life and death, being only saved by the power of a medicine man, who possessed great influence with the spirit of the spring.

The story of the spring, as I have heard it, is that away back, many generations ago, a war of long duration and great bitterness had raged between the Navajos and the Utes. The latter had been severely worsted in the war and had been driven far to the north of the Gila river, which had been the original boundary between the two countries. As last, however, the great Cotero came to be chief of the Utes and in a number of battles, he succeeded in driving the Navajos back to the Gila. Whether this was the result of the superior prowess of Cotero, however, or owing to the death of the great chief of the Navajos, Co-a-hua-ta, appeared to be a matter of great doubt.

Certainly the Navajos had grown greatly to outnumber the Utes and there was much doubt among the wise men of the tribe. A young chief named Tahindra, who had given great promise on account of his bravery and wisdom had succeeded to Co-a-hua-ta. But he had recently married a very beautiful maiden of the Mescalero Apaches and instead of commanding the forces of his tribe in person, he had given up his time since arriving at the chieftainship to enjoying his wealth and the company of his beautiful young wife.

It was decided by Cotero and his counselors that it would be wise to follow up his succession of victories with a proposition for peace. This was not done without the strenuous opposition of Cotero. The wise men of the tribe had powers in matters of this kind and the chief was forced to succumb to their dictates. Cotero was filled with an ambition to not only revenge the defeats which his tribe had sustained, but to conquer the hated Navajos. He assented, however, with apparent willingness, when he found that he could not overcome the objections of the wise men to prolonging the war.

Accordingly, the desire of the Utes for peace was signified to the Navajos and a grand council of the chiefs and wise men of both nations was agreed upon. Cotero and his advisors met with those of Tahindra, but the latter was not present, having remained at home with his wife. The Navajos demanded a large piece of valuable hunting grounds from the Utes, but the latter declared themselves unwilling to grant this or indeed to enter into a treaty if Tahindra were not present. The latter finally consented to appear, but brought with him his wife and family.

When Cotero saw the lovely young wife of Tahindra, he fell desperately in love with her. So deeply did he become enamored of her that he determined to possess her at all hazards. Accordingly, he entered into a plan with some of his braves to steal the woman. At the same time he determined to get rid of his wise men. He became acquainted with the plans of Tahindra and on a day upon which the latter determined to go on a hunt, he also absented himself from camp on some pretext. He arranged with his braves to take possession of Tahindra's wife and to join him a day's journey away. The remainder of the Utes had accompanied Tahindra and as nothing of the kind was expected, the plan was easily carried out. But in their hurry a mistake was made. Instead of Tahindra's wife being taken, her sister, quite as lovely as she, was carried away by the braves, she, herself, aiding in the deception in order to save her sister.

When Tahindra learned what had occurred on his return from the chase, he was wild with rage and had all of the wise men of the Utes put to death with great torture. Cotero was also wild with rage when he found the mistake that had been made, but there was nothing for him to do but go on with what he had so wickedly begun. He proposed to the maiden to marry her, but his proposition was received with scorn and hatred. He determined to make the best use he could of her possession and pushed on to his home. The maiden was imprisoned in this gulch, where it was certain that the Navajos would never find her and Cotero sent word to the Navajos that the maiden would be held until peace was agreed upon and a large part of their territory given him as a ransom. Tahindra, urged on by his wife, waged furious war for the recovery of her sister, but, however false and cruel Cotero may have been, when rid of his counselors, he proved too able a warrior for the Navajos and not only held his own but drove the Navajos far south of the Gila.

The maiden was kept imprisoned in this gulch for a number of years, her food being thrown down to her from the rocks above and drinking from this spring. One night, when hopeless of relief, she attempted to scale these rocks by means of the vines climbing over the spring in an effort to escape, but missed her hold and fell fully a thousand feet back, striking upon this mound, in which her body was buried by the force of the fall."

This concluded the story of Martinez and it was hardly through when he hurried away, so great was his aversion to the spot. I wrapped my blankets about me and lay down to rest, but though weary from the hard march, it was some time before I sunk to sleep. The sad fate of the Indian maiden and the lonely vigils which she must have passed shut up in the gloomy gulch, were in my mind. How long I had slept I have no idea. I awoke from a dream in which I appeared to be drowning, only to find water rushing over me in torrents. I sprang to my feet in alarm. My attention was instantly attracted to the spring. From every one of the fissures of the rock gushed forth a fierce stream of water, accompanied by the most unearthly sounds. Moans, groans and shrieks filled the air. I stood rooted to the ground in astonishment, unable to move hand or foot. I stood spell-bound thus for nearly half an hour, during which the unearthly uproar continued.

Then my attention was arrested by a wild, awful cry, such as I will never forget, which came from above my head. I glanced upward and to my intense horror, I saw descending, a radiant human figure. It came down with fearful velocity and struck the ground immediately in front of me, into which it disappeared. Short as the time was, I could see that it was the form of an Indian woman of great beauty.

Scarcely had the body or spirit, which ever it might be called, disappeared from sight, then the spring began to resume its usual aspect. The sounds died out and the waters ceased to gush forth but I still stood there dripping wet, and spell-bound by what I had seen until with a mighty effort, I roused myself and fled from the scene almost crazed with fright. But my flight was not of long duration as in the darkness I ran over a ledge of rock, falling a considerable distance. One of my legs was broken by the fall and I was forced to lie there until found in the morning by Martinez, who had returned to search for me. He did not appear to be at all surprised at what had happened to me, but like the honest fellow that he was, he assisted me to a considerable distance from the spring and nursed me carefully until I had recovered the use of my limbs sufficiently to leave the gulch."

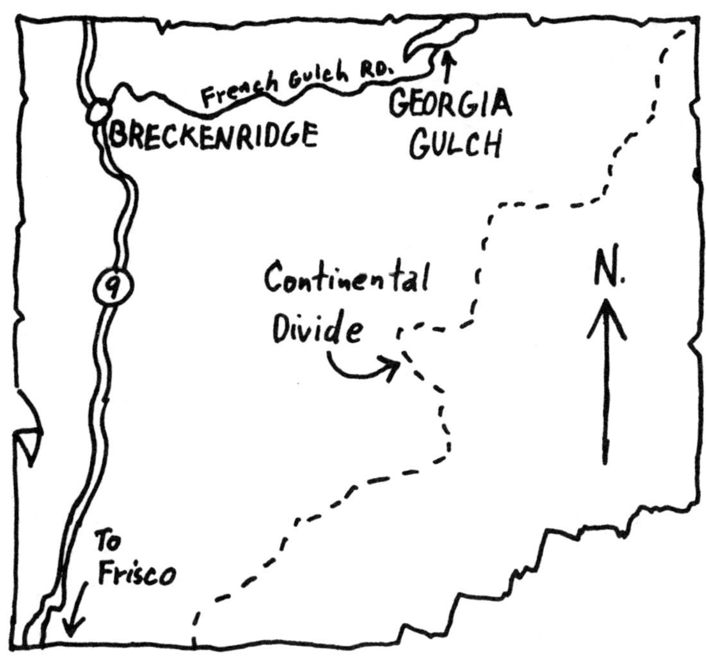

March 30, 1884

Reprinted with the permission of the Rocky Mountain News.

GRASPING A SPIRIT

The Experience
of a Bold Georgetown Woman Who Felt a Phantom Form
Melt Under Her Fingers.

To the Rocky Mountain News.

Georgetown, August 8, - The question has often been asked, "If a materialized spirit would be grabbed by one of the sitters (during a seance), what would be the result?"

In one case of Mrs. Markee, a spirit form was grabbed, but forced itself from the person who acted the bull in the china store and the medium[1] was found covered with blood in the cabinet[2] and has not yet, after two years, fully recovered her health. A genuine case of spirit grabbing, but with less disastrous results, occurred at my house on the evening of July 27, 1881, and an account of it will not only be interesting to the majority of your readers, but also prove to be a valuable contribution to the science of spiritualism.[3]

Mrs. N. D. Miller, of Denver, Colorado, formerly from Memphis, Tennessee, and whose history can be found in Dr. Watson's work "The Clock Struck One," has been, in company with her husband, a welcome visitor at my house and gave us a materializing seance in my parlor on the evening of July 27. There were present, besides myself and wife, the medium and her husband, a well known gentleman from Georgetown, Mr. Cree and a person by the name of Mrs. M. Smith, a powerful woman, who, as the sequel showed, had been hired to attempt an assault, which might have proved not less than an assassination.

The cabinet was formed by a few blankets hung up over a frame in a corner of our room. After the usual physical manifestation had gone through, forms appeared from the cabinet. From thirty to forty materialized forms of all sizes; men, women and children, sometimes two at a time, came out of the same, conversed with the sitters, took them into the cabinet to examine the medium, while other forms walked outside, some of them dematerializing in front of the cabinet and apparently sinking down through the carpeted floor. Most of these forms were recognized and excellent tests were given. One well known lady, who had died a few months ago in Hot Springs, Arkansas, promised to my wife on her death-bed that if it were possible, she would return to her. Of this arrangement nobody in this town knew anything, not even myself.

That evening a spirit form, looking exactly like her, walked out of the cabinet and taking my wife's arm, said, "Didn't I promise to return? Here I am." She also gave her name which was Minnie Bowman, but this was unnecessary, as my wife fully recognized her features.

Towards the end of the seance, one materialized form walked up to Mrs. Smith. When Mrs. Smith beheld the form, she pretended to recognize the same as her deceased mother and with the cry, "Oh, my mother! My mother!" she went, apparently, into hysterics. She grasped the spirit's arms with both of her hands, while she kept on yelling, "Oh, this is my mother. Do not take her away." We all witnessed the struggle of the form, to free itself from the iron grasp of elephantine Mrs. Smith and fearing that some injury might result to the medium, we went to the assistance of the spirit. When we took hold of Mrs. Smith's hands, her fingers were still clinging to the wrists of the spirit form, but these wrists ended in nothing - there was nobody attached to them. Finally, these spirit arms, still held by the grasp of Mrs. Smith's fingers, melted away, too, while Mrs. Smith kept on screaming and was (or pretended to be) too much excited to be reasoned with or quieted down. While this struggle was going on, we all had our heads touched and coats pulled by other spirit hands, while, at the same time, the voice of "Red Face", the Indian, spoke from the cabinet.

Of the many other remarkable occurrences during the seance, I will only mention that the medium's babe had become restless and was taken by a materialized form into the cabinet and there made to nurse, while other spirit forms kept on

appearing and walking the floor. My wife's daughter who died when a child, appeared as a young girl, resembling very much, her still mortal sister. My wife held her hand, the former sank down through the floor, vanishing and reappeared the next moment from the cabinet. A lady friend of mine, who died several years ago in Galveston, Texas, appeared and looked as natural as I ever saw her in life. She also told me her maiden name and the name of her first husband; both of which I found out since to be correct. The other parties present received similar tests. I might go on describing those wonderful things, but all these manifestations have been described in the "Banner of Light" and other papers so often that it would only appear as a repetition of well known facts. All that appears new are the above given facts of spirit-grabbing, the truth of which I herewith most emphatically affirm.

The physiological effects of this spirit-grabbing were not quite as disastrous to Mrs. Miller as they might have been. When the medium was carried out of the cabinet, she was apparently lifeless. No pulse and no heart-beat could be detected. Gradually, both returned, the medium became conscious and complained of great fatigue and nausea at the stomach.

It seems to me the very pinnacle of absurdity to affirm, as some ignorant or evil disposed persons do, that Mrs. Miller could simulate such a condition or produce the above related manifestations herself. Neither do I pretend to be able to explain what those materialized forms really are and how they are produced. Those things I leave to such men as Professors Zoeliner, Crocker, Wallace and others to investigate and explain as science advances. All I can affirm most positively is that during an acquaintance of two years and after several sittings with the Millers, I have found them to be the most honest and unassuming people. They have no desire to deceive - they could not deceive if they wished to do so and there would be no inducement for them to do so. As to my knowledge, a large percentage of their patrons are dead beats. From this class of observers (?) are recruited the army of "exposers" and wiseacres, the calumniators, liars and backbiters. From this class, the Millers have suffered as much as ever martyr suffered in this advanced age. But as every noisome insect fills its place in nature and has some purpose to accomplish, so this class of "exposers" do good without knowing it, by causing a healthy reaction of thought and by exciting the interest of those that are able to think for themselves, until finally the grand fact of immortality of the soul will be more than a mere theological dogma; when the material and spiritual universe will be blended into one harmonious whole and there be light for all.

Yours very respectfully, DR. HARTMANN.

August 14, 1881

Reprinted with the permission of the Rocky Mountain News.

1. A medium is a person who claims to have certain psychic powers that enable them to make con- tact with the spirit world.

2. The cabinet is a tool used by the medium to help harness so-called "psychic energies". It could be as elaborate or as simple as the user wished (in the case of our story, it was a small wood frame with blankets thrown over it).

Usually the medium would enter the cabinet, fall into a trance-like state and "produce" alleged spirit forms that would move about and interact with the observers.

3. Spiritualism is an almost world-wide belief that the soul or spirit, survives after death and that this same soul or spirit can communicate with the living, usually through the aid of a medium.

A HAUNTED HOUSE

The Haunted House in Denver.
How Its Principal "Demon" was Brought to See the Error of Its Ways.
It is Rented by a Medium. - A Stone Thrown. - The Spirits Obdurate.
Most Wonderful Revealments.

The following article is taken from a copy of the Chicago Progressive Thinker of July 14, 1894, and was written by one of Denver's most reliable citizens, and may be relied upon as stating the facts as they occurred. While the HERALD is not much of a believer in things that occur after dark (unless there is something tangible in it), in this case we are convinced there is something to work on. The article says:

TO THE EDITOR - Few persons are able to say truthfully that they know their reputations for truth and veracity in the community in which they reside and those few are generally persons whose reputations are bad and have been made the subject of investigation in a court of justice. For myself, I can only say that I have resided in this community some thirty four years and have never heard my reputation discussed, but have reason to believe that it is good. I intend keeping it so and, but for the fact that the statements I am about to make are substantiated by the testimony of eight other witnesses whose characters have never of my knowledge been attacked, I should now remain silent. It is of the utmost importance that established facts regarding spirit phenomena be told, let the consequences to the narrator be what they may.

Here are the facts as briefly as I am able to state them, though much of a very interesting dialog is left out in order to save space.

Right in the heart of the residence portion of Denver, only a few blocks from the business center and not one hundred feet from a frequently occupied church edifice, there stands, and for the past fifteen years has stood, a neat and well-preserved brick cottage. The inside history of this house I shall not at this time attempt to relate, but during the past six or seven years it has been impossible to keep it tenanted. People have moved in and then moved out with distressing frequency. A vast majority of the people of Denver do not believe in ghosts; at least they so profess and respect for public opinion or the fear of being laughed at, induced most of the persons who had attempted to live in this cottage to supply some other reason for moving than the true one, viz; "The house is haunted." Still from time to time, the story has been "told in confidence," and the reputation of the house became established so that from some time past it has been without a tenant.

There has resided in this city several months, a gentleman well and favorably known to spiritualists throughout the United States as a trumpet medium.[1] This gentleman, Mr. Charles W. Steward, finding the little cottage which he has been occupying becoming too small to accommodate the number of sitters attending his circles, began looking about for more commodious quarters, and in one of his house-hunting tours came upon the cottage in question and being favorably impressed by its external appearance, he obtained a key and proceeded to explore its interior and while thus engaged became aware, through his mediumistic faculties, that there were occupants therein who paid no rent and whom a distress warrant would not reach. Brief inquiry in the neighborhood acquainted him with the reputation of the house. He forthwith sought the agent and was soon placed in possession of the premises at a very moderate rent.

Mr. Steward has a development class, composed principally of gentlemen and when he reported what he had done, it was at once suggested, moved and carried that the class proceed to the cottage and hold a seance.

On the evening of June 21st, at about 8 o'clock, seven gentlemen of the class, accompanied by Prof. Steward and Miss Coldren, another powerful trumpet medium, "might have been seen wending their silent way" to the haunted house. Arrived there, the first thing in order was a most thorough examination of the premises from cellar to roof. This being accomplished and the house being found absolutely vacant (there being nothing in the way of furniture except a rickety old chair) the party entered a small bedroom situated in the front part of the house - a room about 7 by 9 feet in size, having one window and one door. The chair referred to had been taken into this room for the use of the young lady medium.

Just after the members of the circle had gotten into the small room and while the writer was standing in the doorway between this room and the parlor, speaking to Prof. Steward, who was just inside the bedroom, a sharp and loud report as of some very hard and heavy substance striking the floor with great force was heard. Immediately thereafter, loud raps were heard upon the chair in which Miss Coldren was seated; the the chair was moved with considerable violence and Miss Coldren concluded to stand up with the rest of the circle.

The door being closed, the room was quite dark, as but little light came through the window, which was provided with heavy outside blinds. About this time it was discovered that no trumpet had been brought along, the Professor saying that he had not been told to bring any and did not think one would be required.

While Prof. Steward was talking, another voice, deep and strong, was heard, coming apparently from under the floor. This voice asked, "What are you people doing here?"

Someone replied, "We are here for the purpose of becoming acquainted with you."

Voice; "Well, you had better get out."

Reply; "No, sir, we will not get out until we have accomplished what we came to do."

V. "Well, who in h__l are you, anyway?"

R. "We are friends of yours and of all other spirits who need help."

V. "D___n you, I don't want your help. I want you to get out of this house."

R. "Mr. Spirit, you can't frighten us. We did not come here to bulldoze you, and you can't bulldoze us."

V. "_____ ______you, if you don't get out of here in twenty minutes, I'll pull the d____d house down on your heads."

R. "Spirit, you cannot frighten us by swearing. We came here to do good and here we are going to remain. We also intend moving into this house and living here."

V. "Do you think you can drive me out?"

R. "Oh, no. We don't want to drive you out. We want you to stay here so that we can get acquainted with you."

V. "This is my house and you people want to drive me out so you can get my money!"

R. "No, spirit. You are wrong. We don't want your money and if you realize that you are a spirit, you ought to know that you can have no use for money. Do you know that you are now on the spirit side of life?"

V. "Yes, I know all about that."

R. "Then you ought to know that we cannot harm you."

V. "I know. Well, you can't hurt me, but I can hurt you if you don't get out of here soon."

R. "Now, spirit, be reasonable. Let us talk together without anger. We would like to know who you are."

V. "It's none of your business. Now get out of this house."

And so the dialogue proceeded for several minutes, until someone asked him if he wanted us to sing. The voice replied that there was a church across the street where they were singing all the time. He was told that we did not sing church songs

and finally he consented to listen while we sang a simple spiritual song. After the singing, the spirit became milder in his language and presently said, "Well, you seem to be pretty good sort of people and I am sorry I threw that stone at you."

Question; "Where did you get the stone?"

Voice; "I got it out of the pantry in the back room."

Q. "Are there any other spirits in this house?"

V. "Yes, lots of them. The boys are up stairs, playing cards now."

Q. "Can't you bring them down so we can talk to them?"

V. "No, I won't. I'm boss here. If you have anything to say, you can talk to me. There are enough spirits here now."

After several other questions had been asked by members of the circle and answered by the spirit in a manner not altogether satisfactory, the voice suddenly asked, "Who is that old man over there?" He was told that the gentleman was Mr. Crass, who had been a soldier.

Voice; "What regiment did you belong to?"

Mr. Crass replied to this, giving name and number of his army corps, division, battalion, regiment and company.

Voice; "I saw you at Lookout Mountain, Mr. Crass."

Mr. C. "Is that so? Well, I was there."

V. "When I saw you last, your feet were swollen so you couldn't walk."

Mr. C. "Well, well, that is all true. I had to go to the hospital."

V. "Are you a spiritualist, too?"

Mr. C. "Yes, I am."

V. "I'm going home with you."

Mr. C. "All right. You are welcome. I have a trumpet there and my spirit friends will teach you how to use it."

V. "Trumpet! What's that for?"

The use of a trumpet was explained.

V. "I don't want anything to talk through. I can talk without a horn."

At this point it was suggested by Prof. Steward that we sing "Home Sweet Home." When the song had been sung, the voice said, "I had a home once, but was robbed of it." He was told that if he would come with us he would be given a home better and brighter than any he had ever known but for some time the spirit remained obdurate and insisted that we were trying to play some trick upon him. The singing had, however, produced a great change in the character of his language and eventually, his stubbornness was broken down and he consented to return with us to Prof. Steward's home.

After the spirit had begun to talk in a milder tone, a small circle of bright light was seen floating over our heads. This was interpreted by Prof. Steward to mean that the spirit was to be invited to join our circle. We shortly adjourned to the residence of Prof. Steward and formed our customary trumpet circle, whereupon all the guides and controls[2.] forthwith began a jubilee which was kept up for several minutes. After a time, the rejoicing having calmed down, Johnny Cummings, who is in the principal control of Prof. Steward, announced that our new friend would try to use the trumpet and presently the late "demon of the haunted house" began talking in a whisper saying, "Oh, friends, friends, you don't know how much good you have done to-night. I am so happy! I can't talk much now, but if you let me, I will come again. This is all new to me. I can't understand it yet, but I thank you friends and will come again."

The controls told us that they had not been able to see this spirit until they had gotten him within our circle and they are still unable to explain how he had managed to talk without the assistance of a medium or trumpet in that vacant house. It was something new to them and they would try to find out how it was done and, if possible, explain to us. They congratulated us upon the results of the evenings work and assured us that we should never have cause to regret it.

It is not expected that this narration of facts will convince any unbeliever, but it may induce some doubting Thomas to investigate and it may also convey a hint as to the proper method of dealing with those discontented spirits who appear to take delight in tormenting people who know nothing concerning a spiritual existence and whose chief employment in spirit-life is found in "giving a house a bad name."

Anyone in Denver being the possessor of a "haunted house," and desiring to have the objectionable tenants ejected, can be accommodated free of cost by applying to any member of Professor Steward's development class. When Professor and Mrs. Steward move into their new home, we expect to have great times with "the boys" who meet there to play cards and hold high carnival.

Aug. 11, 1894

Rocky Mountain Herald

1. The trumpet was a long megaphone-like instrument allegedly used by the spirit to speak through during a seance.

2. Guides or controls were spirits which helped other spirits to communicate with the medium during a seance.